Teaching
Macbeth
(and More)

Teaching Macbeth (and More)

Better Planning, Better Learning

Dan Flickstein

CORWIN PRESS, INC.
A Sage Publications Company
Thousand Oaks, California

For information address:

Corwin Press, Inc.
2455 Teller Road
Thousand Oaks, California 91320
e-mail: order@corwin.sagepub.com

SAGE Publications Ltd.
6 Bonhill Street
London EC2A 4PU
United Kingdom

SAGE Publications India Pvt. Ltd.
M-32 Market
Greater Kailash I
New Delhi 110 048 India

Printed in the United States of America

Library of Congress Cataloging-in-Publication Data

Flickstein, Dan.
    Teaching Macbeth (and more): Better planning, better learning /
author, Dan Flickstein.
        p. cm.
    Includes bibliographical references.
    ISBN 0-8039-6390-4   (acid-free paper). — ISBN 0-8039-6391-2 (pbk.:
    acid-free paper)
    1. Literature—Study and teaching (Secondary)   I. Title.
PN59.F55   1996
807'.1'2—dc20   95–50182

This book is printed on acid-free paper.

96 97 98 99 10 9 8 7 6 5 4 3 2 1

Corwin Production Editor: Gillian Dickens

Contents

Preface

Although all my career as a teacher of English and speech has been devoted to a large urban high school in New York City, it remains my assumption that the pages of this manual easily translate to large urban high schools across America. Moreover, these pages should serve as a useful tool to any teacher of the communication arts about to embark on the instruction of lengthy literary works to adolescents in a large or small setting, be it urban or rural.

A resource section has been included that contains three sets of lesson plans that follow techniques described in the explanatory text. The reader is not to assume that such lesson plans are for sale or that their creator has maintained a file of other plans that are for sale, barter, or to be relinquished in any other manner. That would, in fact, be counter to the philosophy that went into the preparation herein discussed. The English teacher, to perfect his or her style, must do personal preparation for growth. Three sets of lessons were included because of the variations involved and because each set proved successful when used in the classroom. Lessons on *Nectar in a Sieve* are of the collaborative style. *The Scarlet Letter* was included to demonstrate how a difficult text can be taught to pupils in the 11th grade. *Macbeth* lessons exhibit additional research demanded of a gifted class of pupils. All lessons, I hope, display methods that require as much as possible from the young minds to which they are directed.

Acknowledgments

Many years have passed since I studied a college course considering methods of how to teach oral communication skills to high school students. I remember little now of what my professors said in the classroom or of what the textbook—we did have one—professed to be effective for teaching adolescents the speech arts. Perhaps it is good that I've forgotten because so very much has changed in education since 1966, the year I graduated from Brooklyn College and obtained, in September, my first teaching license. Yet what I do remember from my methods course that has served me well during my 29+–year career as a teacher of speech and English on the secondary level in the New York City Board of Education is the seriousness and care with which the experts at Brooklyn College taught. They were meticulous about "dotting the i's" and handling the proverbial "p's and q's." They were insistent that understanding and knowledge be part of a teacher's foundation because of the importance of what teachers do. They maintained a rigorous work ethic that they would not alter. For that I sincerely thank them.

I owe much more gratitude to my supervisors over the course of my career, all of whom were equally caring and diligent, beginning with my first chairman of the English Department of Abraham Lincoln High School, Jack M. Pollock (who eventually served as the school's principal for more than 20 years), and extending to Norma Tasman, former chairperson of English at Brooklyn's Sheepshead Bay High School; Martin Salkin, former chairperson of Speech and later of English at Abraham Lincoln High School; Irma Weiss, former assistant-principal-supervision/English at Abraham Lincoln High School and present assistant-principal-supervision/English at the Bronx High School of Science; and Rosemarie Buonomo, current assistant-principal-supervision/English at Abraham Lincoln High School.

Even more, I thank many of my colleagues from whom I have learned throughout the years, including the late Jerry Fishman, wonderfully bright and creative Jim Mangano and Art Cooper, equally creative and patient Mel Glenn, and phenomenally insightful and well-read Howard Wallach and his wife, Betty.

Additional gratitude goes to my aunt, Eve Goldfarb, whose own 30+-year career as a dedicated, caring, intelligent English educator served to help me in my quest for excellence, and to her son, my cousin, Richard Goldfarb, also a teacher of English and acting administrator at Junior High School 293 in Brooklyn. I thank him for always listening to me and for imparting to me nothing but wisdom. These people have been both my inspiration and my source material in the creation of this manual.

Finally, I thank my wife, Sandra Flickstein, for the many hours she took from her own busy schedule to finalize the manuscript and to persist in encouraging me to complete the project.

About the Author

Dan Flickstein—In early infancy—or at least as far back as I can remember—amid crying and uttering sounds resembling "mama" and "dada," I said something akin to "I want to teach adolescents in a high school setting." I was extremely fortunate to have lived at a time when Brooklyn College provided both a free and highly regarded education. Its specialty was turning bright young men and women into teachers. I became a teacher in 1966 at Lincoln High, where I have taught my entire career except for 1 year—my second in the business—when I was at neighboring Sheepshead Bay High School. In addition, I have spent 25 years as an adjunct lecturer in the Department of Speech at Brooklyn College. In both places of employment, I was blessed by being surrounded with mentors who were both well intentioned and remarkably intelligent. It was they who helped mold me into the successful educator I am today.

I am the son of hardworking parents who never went to college but who never let me believe I wouldn't go to college. Though divorced in 1976, I spent a great deal of time with my beloved daughters, Amy, now 27 and married to Mr. Darren Schulman, and Nancy, now 25. They were the greatest part of my private life and continue to occupy a major place in my *raison d'être*. In 1986, I remarried. My wife, Sandy, is a demanding physical therapist who complements my life perfectly by greatly admiring the things I do well, while encouraging me to see past my limitations.

1

Planning Lessons on Literature

New York City teachers of all subjects had, in the 1980s, been inundated, either through methods courses or by their supervisors, with the concept of lesson planning: aim, instructional objective, motivation, activity, medial summary, activity, final summary, conclusion, homework assignment. Yet applying this jargon to the actual procedure of preparing lessons is an abstract task—particularly for the creative mind, which is most often the case with a teacher of English.

Why the Need for Such a Book

In training more than a dozen student teachers of English and speech, officially mentoring two, and observing several new teachers in my one-time capacity as department coordinator, I have come across only one who was acquainted with technique in lesson preparation and none who was especially effective in its long-range presentation.

1

It seems that there has not been much printed material available on how to approach the teaching of a lengthy piece of worthy literature. The task of preparing a difficult novel or play for study can surely seem gargantuan in its proportions. How does one begin teaching *Moby Dick*? What should one include or exclude in teaching *Hamlet* or *Macbeth*? How long should it take to teach *Crime and Punishment*? What do I want to teach my students about and from *Cry, the Beloved Country, The Good Earth, Death of a Salesman*, or *Native Son*?

How, indeed, does a new teacher make these decisions? We assume that the teacher has studied literature in both high school and college and has an affinity for literature's wealth of interpretations. We further assume that any teacher of English is both a reader and observer of literature's infinite elements. From this point new teachers of English begin their approach to discover ways to make adolescents read and learn from literature.

Thus the need for the material contained herein stems from the monumental task of preparing a major work of literature, the general lack of regimentation of teachers of the arts, and the paucity of available information on the subject. Although the pages of this text are designed for the novice teacher, they may serve also to refresh experienced minds regarding helpful techniques long forgotten or abandoned.

To Lesson Plan or Not to Lesson Plan

I have come to realize that the need to plan lessons varies with the individual. Known as a planner and notorious list maker among colleagues and family, I used to have single lesson plans that were literally pages in length. When I matured in the education profession, my plans diminished to approximately a page to a page and a half each. Most now are about a page long. Some, usually new plans, I need to make frequent reference to while executing them in the classroom. Others, although they accompany me to class, remain unviewed during the period, except while copying from them the aim and homework assignment included at the beginning and end of the plans.

Adjustments to these older plans occur with regularity, based on a new insight I may have or one (as is usually the case) made by one of my students. Also, as years pass, parts of a plan become outmoded as new events become more relevant than old and as new literature is written, plays staged, movies produced, speeches delivered, and poetry created.

Whether to have lesson plans at all has been hotly debated by New York City faculties, supported by their union and against New York City administrations for years. In the 1980s, when New York City education was mandated to run by "managerial" objectives (similar to the way businesses are run), having a "bona fide" lesson plan for each lesson taught was a prerequisite for a teacher before entering a classroom. Many supervisors, after observing a satisfactory lesson, were taught to reverse their thinking upon discovering that the observed teacher had performed "sans" plan. An unsatisfactory rating would result for the "unprepared" teacher.

As a certified and licensed candidate for assistant-principal-supervision/English since 1984, I underwent frequent questioning in interviews regarding my philosophy of lesson planning and what should be included in a good plan. It was a New York City Board of Education regulation for each teacher to have a lesson plan for every lesson taught. Refusal by a teacher to comply could result in unsatisfactory ratings and eventual termination of employment. Yet when once pressed, I heard a former New York City principal respond to the question of lesson planning as follows: "There are a few very gifted people who are confined by a lesson plan and teach better without one."

This feeling of confinement is what many artistic people reject about the plan. It hampers creativity, stifles spontaneity, and destroys original thinking from those whom we most want to think—the students. "I don't use a 'plan,' " said one highly successful teacher, "just marginal notes in my text and a homework assignment at the end of the section we study for the day." Another very competent colleague said, "I've not looked at my plans for years. Certain things happen in the class as they come to me."

Since the onset of the 1990s, such remarks have become acceptable to New York City administrations because the requirement of a formal daily "managerial" type plan has been abandoned. A lesson plan, still a Board of Education requirement, is now regarded as a personal document and need not follow any set of standard criteria.

Certainly, plans are personal. On more than one occasion, while subbing early in my career, I attempted to teach from lesson plans made by colleagues who were excellent teachers. Because I could follow neither the logic nor the insights of the plans' creators, I was not able to present the lessons effectively.

My preference, having evaluated the pros and cons of planning, is to plan diligently and at length, especially for the new teacher. The job of an English teacher in a high school instructing five classes of over 30 pupils per class and handling clerical work for a homeroom class of another 30+ pupils often precludes imaginative, impromptu thinking. In addition, new teachers (in the midst of philosophical idealism) being instructed in pedagogy often neglect consideration of any or all of the following: absenteeism, poor discipline, emergencies, PA announcements, and department requirements. Add to this the collection of homework, tests, and essays, which seems unending, and a good lesson plan may help to keep a new teacher's head above water during the initial years.

In fact, how can teachers, despite their competence and experience, remember the aim of a lesson, the pages to be analyzed, or the homework assignment, including pages to be read, vocabulary to be studied, and questions to be considered, without having something written down somewhere? How will teachers know when they might use a school's audiovisual aid? The plan should and will assist the teacher in using time economically and in establishing and maintaining routines and discipline. Students get bored, restless, even obstreperous while waiting for a teacher who is fumbling, searching for ideas, or inventing aims or assignments impromptu. They become both perplexed and angry when aim and assignment are not forthcoming. They recognize incompetence, lack of preparedness, and laziness quickly. Good planning helps avoid this. Moreover, good planning will cause teachers to scrutinize two important elements that will make them better teachers—the information (in this case, literature) and the students' behavior.

Should all teachers lesson plan? " 'Tis a consummation devoutly to be wished."[1]

Note

1. Shakespeare, W. (1957). *Hamlet.* New York: Simon & Schuster, p. 63.

2

Keeping the Students Clearly in Mind

A good rhetorician knows that the audience dictates the persuasive methods chosen by the speaker. Consider, therefore, that pupils are an audience. Lesson plans must include aims, motivations, questions, and assignments that pupils can understand, that offer challenge, and that offer substantial opportunities for success. Therefore, we must take into account the following about pupils before beginning to plan: age and grade level, intelligence level, cultural background, socioeconomic condition, and number of pupils on register and in attendance. Such knowledge should help a teacher while planning to teach literature to today's high school student.

Age and Grade Level

Depending on how it is handled, any literature can be taught to any class. Hardy's *Tess of the D'Urbervilles*, for example, can be taught to 14-year-olds and to 18-year-olds, depending on what the teacher expects and ultimately presents. For example, some of the symbolic concepts involved in the descriptive prose might be better directed to an older group, whereas a younger one might more easily focus on the pure love relationship between Angel and Tess. Hardy's vocabulary presents difficulty for most high school students and pupil age is, therefore, less likely to be an issue in selecting it to be taught.

On the other hand, Miller's *Death of a Salesman* contains nearly no new words for vocabulary growth. Yet its content revolves around issues more likely to be studied by older pupils, usually seniors: aging processes, modern tragedy, fate, free will, and determinism. Many schools will supply a new teacher with literature selections suitable for each grade. Departures should not be made from such lists, if only to prevent possible repetition of the literature in another grade, when different literature is to be introduced to increase pupil experience.

Intelligence Level

There are so very many ways by which to judge a person's intelligence that it seems unfair to categorize people by this factor. What we call intelligence has so many interpretations that it tends to be insulting to some, because although they are intelligent, they are not grouped with the "most intelligent," for example, the English "honor" class. Indeed, the insult may be a reality, though unintended. I have heard pupils read well who cannot write a decent sentence. Others conceptualize beautifully but cannot read well. Still others read, write, and conceptualize with insight but fail to achieve success because of any one or a combination of other factors, including poor work habits, frequent lateness or absence, limited attention span, and psychological problems related to the home or adolescence.

Are some students smarter than others? Sure they are! Some are certainly better in English than others because they've read more, or they have talent in writing because of a gifted imagination or an ability to use words. Some speak better owing to better natural voice anatomy, less inhibition, or better research skills. Still others retain gifted insight in observation of human behavior, that is, literature. Educators have made efforts, based on standardized tests and success in subject matter in school, to group pupils so a teacher will know better how to plan and deliver lessons to them. Current theory, however, opposes the "grouping" concept in deference to the idea that all pupils have intelligence rendering them capable of learning at high levels and that given the highest level of learning, youngsters will rise to the occasion.

The same principle that applies to age applies to intelligence: Depending on how subject matter is handled, any literature can be taught to any intelligence level. Hawthorne's *The Scarlet Letter*, generally regarded as difficult reading because of its stilted 19th-century style, extensive vocabulary, and mature concepts focusing on hypocrisy in colonial America, contains many descriptive passages. I have personally experienced a good share of success in discussing *The Scarlet Letter* with 11th-grade students.

In summary, regarding intelligence level—or the ability of pupils to read and write—the teacher must prepare assignments that afford a measure of success yet offer a challenge both to stimulate thinking and to raise it to its highest potential.

Cultural, Socioeconomic Background

Many of our pupils in the City of New York have been raised in cultures and conditions totally foreign to those in the literature we teach. With "multiculturalism" a byword for today's educator, the instructor of English who is planning to teach literature must remain astutely aware that many of the traditions of, for example, the Day family in *Life With Father*, are not readily recognizable to students who hail from Pakistan or China—or who have experienced the trauma of having lived in Vietnam or Cambodia during the 1980s. Moreover, how do our American blacks find relevance in the European tragedy that overcomes the Danish Hamlet? (For that matter, are American whites able to relate to the Dane any better?) In fact, can any of our 1990s adolescents find any familiarity in such a play, when so many have been raised in single-parent homes without ever having known a father? When we select literature involving the upper economic class, like Fitzgerald's *The Great Gatsby*, can our pupils, particularly those who come to school hungry or who, more often than we'd care to admit, live in squalid conditions, find enjoyment and challenge in it?

The answer is, again, a resounding "yes" to all. But the teacher must remember to build into the lessons questions that incorporate universals—concepts that humanity will forever face: friendship, parent-child relationships, love, duty, freedom, honor, dignity, pride, loyalty, truth, and so forth. All cultures, all classes recognize these, and teachers of literature must be cognizant of this in the planning stages. In fact, the best of teachers, knowing their pupils during each semester, might actually direct questions to various groups or to individuals. This will underscore that these universals do exist in all cultures and classes, despite vast differences in tradition, religion, philosophy, and outlook.

Class Size

The smaller class is always the luckier because individual attention to each pupil's skills is better achieved. Teachers with a class of 10 or 15 students can decide, during preparation, who will be called on for various tasks: reading aloud, writing on the board, responding to specific questions, leading a group effort, and so forth. But even in a larger class, some attention should be given to such selection during the planning stages once teachers know their pupils' abilities.

Moreover, because there is usually less opportunity for disruption in a smaller class, the teacher may plan to assist pupil writing on an individual basis right into the actual lesson, while giving other less needy pupils another assignment that may be reviewed at home. In smaller classes, teachers are, in general, more likely to collect work for checking at home. Size of class, in my opinion, calls for individual attention to be built into the plan when student numbers are reduced to 15 or fewer.

Other Factors

Nothing is more important in education than the people who are being educated. But other factors do exist when considering preparation for teaching a lengthy piece of literature. For example, a good curriculum in English always requires the educator to teach skills in reading, writing, speaking, and listening, which necessitates learning of fundamentals. This takes time!

But how much time can be devoted to one piece of literature—a week (5 days), a month (20 days)—before we interfere with other matter essential to an entire English course? Educators differ on this. Some say no single piece of literature should take more than 2 weeks (10 lessons) to complete, to afford pupils opportunity to study additional books. Others insist they cannot do justice to a masterwork in fewer than 25 lessons, plus tests at strategic points. They add that such intensive study is worthwhile in lieu of teaching, during one semester, several pieces in less depth.

Department regulations and school wealth, however, may help the English instructor decide how many lessons may be used to teach one book. If, for example, a school has 300 senior students divided into 10 classes of 30 each and each teacher would like to teach *Othello*, problems arise if there are fewer than 300 available copies of the text, which is never *not* the case. The books must be shared, each teacher having access to them for a given period of time.

Once the decision is made on approximately how many lessons will be used, the instructor must also constantly keep in mind the length of time of each individual lesson and, further, how long each homework assignment will take a pupil in the class to complete. A 40-minute period typically exists for high school students in New York City day high schools and a 45-minute nightly assignment is considered not unreasonable (by educators, not students).

In addition, educators might consider their own needs in selecting what to teach and how to prepare it. Surely each teacher has individual strengths and pupils may profit by the teacher incorporating such abilities into the literature (e.g., speaking assignments such as debate, news reporting such as creating a class newspaper on a book, presenting part of a play, etc.).

To sum up what to consider in planning before ever placing ink on paper (or fingers on computer), remember the pupils first and foremost, then the time constraints, and finally the individual personal abilities and talents of the teacher.

3

Studying Literature
Why Bother?

Before embarking on specifics on how to create lesson plans, still more prefatory material is essential to build a foundation for understanding the lesson plan's nature. There is no use in writing a plan merely to occupy 40 minutes of time or to satisfy a mundane regulation. The plan must have reason, purpose—it is a guide to achieve an end. These ends are what the next several pages will address, including logical thinking, values clarification, reading for understanding and appreciation, writing improvement, increasing vocabulary skills, clear speaking, effective listening, basis for communication and understanding among peers, and increase in active responsibility.

Logical, Creative Thinking

More important than any other reason for teaching literature is the development in a pupil of a logical mind and an active imagination.

In that regard, the objective of the high school literature teacher is the same as the high school mathematics teacher, except, of course, that one deals with words and the other with numbers. Consider that a literature teacher asks questions about an event, a theme, a choice of word, an image, and so forth. The desired response must have a logical base and, more to the point, needs to be supported by direct reference to the literature. Teenagers should be able to say that their answers are reflected in the text under discussion by referring to specific incidents, pages, or even lines. If a question is more open-ended, references to other literature or personal experiences need to be included. Personal examples or analogies from real life to literature also serve to bolster logic. In this way, the mind may become and remain adroit, like a gymnast's body that must be toned and constantly conditioned.

Understanding and Appreciation

Logical thinking should help produce young readers who are able to understand what they read while classes explore the various elements of literature. But mere understanding of the "spitback" variety is not nearly enough. Adolescents are capable of deep emotion. They readily love or hate. These emotions and others should be brought into play when forming opinions about authors' styles and techniques. Pupils should be taught to use their logic in determining how literature evokes emotional response. For example, knowing that Hamlet never liked Claudius, students can be expected to form conclusions about how Hamlet will react when in the presence of Claudius, especially in light of the fact that Claudius becomes Hamlet's stepfather in addition to being his natural uncle. The teacher may further challenge pupils to explain how the playwright compelled the audience to continue reading or viewing, in this case, *Hamlet*. In addition, appreciation of time spent, research, descriptive passages— the very art form—should undergo special emphasis. One cannot teach, for example, *The Old Man and the Sea* well without regard for its Christian symbolism or *Tess of the D'Urbervilles* without regard for its inclusion of descriptive passages mirroring feelings and climate. The high school student must be brought to the point of insight and then asked to make honest assessments based on personal reactions.

That is part of critical thinking, development of individual taste, and motivation for creative imagination.

Vocabulary, Writing, Speaking, Listening

All aspects of teaching English, not only literature, incorporate exercises for the improvement of writing, speaking, and listening skills. Thus far, in this text, reading and internal logic have been emphasized. But in preparing literature lessons for teenage children, challenges must be offered to increase their vocabularies, thereby improving their writing, speaking, and listening abilities and also their reading. Although considerable good literature exists in which vocabulary is limited, for example, Arthur Miller's plays, among others, it is incumbent on the teacher to select other matter that provides in-depth vocabulary study; authors such as Edith Wharton, James Baldwin, and, of course, Shakespeare should not by any means be avoided but, instead, selected and scrutinized.

Lessons should provide pupils with writing challenges ranging from brief reactions to creative paragraphs to full-length essays. For example, students may be asked to write a brief reaction to the conclusion of Wright's *Native Son* or, at the end of any lesson, could be called on to write about what point was brought out during the period. They could be challenged to rewrite what might have happened in *Romeo and Juliet* had Mercutio not intervened on Romeo's behalf. They might even be required to compare economic conditions from Hansbury's *A Raisin in the Sun* to those in Williams's *The Glass Menagerie*. Important to any type of writing assignment involving literature is reference to or direct quotes from the text or texts under analysis.

Both vocabulary lessons and writing assignments provide the need for pupils to listen to instructions, but literature lessons need to go beyond that. Provision should be made whereby pupils studying novels, biographies, and so forth are expected to listen not only to the teacher in the classical Socratic question-answer discovery technique but to each other. They should be offered assignments in groups, during which time each member contributes toward a group reaction and presentation. A spokesperson from this group then offers the group's ideas to the entire class, which should respond to the group's performance in both speaking and writing. The group may also be requested to place a written response on the board for class scrutiny and note taking. Classes might also require oral reading, debate, acting, public speaking, or other speaking assignments as exercises in logic, confidence building, and other goals of oral communication.

Values Clarification

In the middle and late 1980s, urban societies raised a cry for help because children seemed to be losing a sense of what is important in life. It became vital then to use the literature teachers present to adolescents to stress values. The problem that arises is, of course, what values should be taught. I presume that even the most liberal thinkers would not find it unreasonable to regard life as sacred and respect for one's fellow humans as essential for a society to exist. In much literature that has survived, there are events or episodes of exemplary human decency to emulate or themes and plots emphasizing decay, human inadequacies, and horror from which to learn prevention and avoidance.

Even novels such as Orwell's *1984* or Golding's *Lord of the Flies* can be used to stress the beauty of mankind. Although the teacher's job is not to distort the viewpoint of the author (e.g., Golding's view of the beast in man), the teacher of adolescents can surely ask the class to offer examples from life and from other literature (e.g., Paton's *Cry, the Beloved Country*; Wilder's *Our Town*; Shakespeare's tragedies) that ennoble humankind.

Although preaching is to be avoided and proselytizing is taboo, there seems every good reason to emphasize what is positive about being alive—and this need not be done only through the works of a writer such as Walt Whitman but also through the works of writers of economically deprived characters, such as Toni Morrison or even a nihilist such as Samuel Beckett.

Elevating the Level of Peer Discussion

It seems not unreasonable to assume that adolescents converse among themselves about sports, the opposite sex, movies, and television. Within this narrow choice of topics exist issues of importance ranging from justice, fair play, and honor, to attempts to understand the nature of relationships and even the improvement of the human condition. Literature, however, broadens adolescents' perspective. Literature allows them to form conclusions about concepts, people, and environments different from, yet similar to, their own; for example, the love and persistence of Jay Gatsby, the dogged yet dignified struggles of Markandaya's family in *Nectar in a Sieve,* or Macbeth fighting his own ambition and resulting guilt.

By giving pupils the common thread of having read the same literature, the youngsters become able to weave theories about life new to them. Their experiences and curiosity tend to grow and they develop increased insight into their personal lives, for which they could previously offer only clichés and platitudes.

Increase in Responsibility

In my experience some pupils will work very hard to understand literature, some will work merely to fulfill an obligation, and some will not work at all. Yet my assignments have always remained the type that demand time and thinking because my experience has taught me that when I expect more, I get more. When I expect little, that is what I get. A part of teaching literature that is similar to teaching all subject matter is to make the student a more responsible person. Homework should be given and done regularly. Pupils should be prepared with it for each lesson. Moreover, pupils should be ready to respond in class to a teacher's questions and to responses offered by peers with facts and opinions supported by references to the required reading. Ideally, pupils should be motivated not only by their personal interest in the literature but also by their individual sense of responsibility to both themselves and the class as a whole, for everyone to benefit from literary activities guided by the teacher.

Reading Literature
Is an Active Experience

I have frequently compared for my pupils the mind of a logical thinker to the body of a conditioned athlete. If either stops exercising, solid, useful tissue grows into flabby, unhealthy fat. When we do not exercise our logic, it will not remain cogent. Our late 20th-century (especially urban-dwelling) adolescents have been raised on a steady and heavy diet of television watching, which requires mainly passive behavior, especially when compared to the activity reading a book demands. Thus it is incumbent on English instructors to keep students' minds sharp and alert in conjunction with all the other important reasons that literature should be studied in high schools.

4

Learning Lessons About Lessons
What Makes a Good Plan?

Although a traditional lesson plan format certainly exists, it is frequently shunned by experienced teachers. Creative people, especially, feel cloistered by the confines of categories and lockstep methodology. But for many teachers, new and experienced—and for me—the standard lesson plan format works remarkably well. The format includes the following steps every day:

Aim
Behavioral objective
Motivation
Activity
Medial summary
Activity
Final summary and conclusion
Homework assignment

Each of these steps will now be analyzed and exemplified.

Aims

The aim of a lesson, or what teachers want their students to know once the lesson is completed, serves a twofold purpose. The aim is written on the board, usually in the form of a question, and elicited from students. The first purpose of the aim is to clarify for pupils what they will be learning for the period. Because literature, unlike mathematics or spelling, is subjective and so often intangible, it is important that students are aware of their focus for the day. In this way the pupil may mentally unclutter the many ideas a book offers, while underscoring particular issues under discussion or writing techniques employed by the author. Some argue that such "uncluttering" narrows and stifles a youngster's natural reactions and understanding. I have come to learn that this is rare. Most people I've taught need an atomizing of literary works to help them zero in on subtleties not easily perceived otherwise. Seeing an aim in front of them gives them some comfort and sheds some light on what may be many obscure areas of potential interest.

The aim of a lesson has equal importance to the teacher. After reading a lengthy masterwork, such as Dostoevsky's *Crime and Punishment,* a new teacher is likely to be more than perplexed about how to begin preparing a lesson, with questions concerning what to teach from the novel, how many lessons to prepare, and so forth. All these are vital concerns and will be addressed in this text. But the purpose (or aim) of this section is to explain the use of an aim, convince the reader of its value, and convince the reader to use an aim. After excusing this somewhat heavy-handed example, the teacher will understand that an aim helps keep him from "wandering."

When established, an aim can, I have found, cause the remainder of a creative lesson to fall into place. Returning to *Crime and Punishment* for a moment, I believe the novice teacher may feel the need to evaluate Sonja in the face of her employment in the world's "oldest profession." The aim may be internally worded (said to yourself) as follows: "I want my students to sympathize with Sonja's reasons for becoming a prostitute," but phrased in question form on the board for the pupils as "Why did Sonja become a prostitute?" In this way pupils are not forced to agree with your sympathetic viewpoint if they do not care to. They should be taught, however, to support intelligently any alternative opinion.

Aims should not only help a student to focus and a teacher to narrow the lesson's goal. Other criteria exist for creating a worthwhile aim. For example, as I just argued, the aim must not trap a pupil into voicing the teacher's interpretation. Although it may allow the pupil to perceive and appreciate the teacher's view, the aim must allow original, critical thinking from the pupil.

Moreover, the aim must have intrinsic worth. The aim must consist of something pupils can study, examine, and scrutinize and about which they can form opinions. The aim must be something that will improve their abilities to read better, write better, speak better, and listen better—in other words, improve their abilities to communicate!

The aim must also be devoid of hatred and prejudice. Although it is impossible not to have our biases about literature and life sneak into our English lessons, a good, honest teacher should take care to label editorial comments and personal interpretations and to accept opposing thought, provided that it is logically derived and supported.

A sampling of aims worded as questions for various literature lessons follows:

1. What evidence suggests Biff and Happy Loman are mature?
2. How does Shakespeare make Claudius sympathetic in Act III, Scene 3 of *Hamlet*?
3. How do Edith Wharton's descriptive passages enhance the suspense between Ethan and Mattie?
4. What similarities exist between the people and the robots in the first act of Capek's *RUR*?
5. What environmental factors influenced Bigger Thomas to become a murderer?
6. What are Atticus's reasons for agreeing to defend Tom Robinson?
7. What purposes does the Stage Manager serve in Wilder's *Our Town*?
8. What family tensions does Hansbury introduce in the first scene of *A Raisin in the Sun*?
9. What flirtations occur between Stanley and Blanche when they first meet?

10. To what extent has Lady Macbeth provoked Macbeth to murder Duncan?

A final word about aims concerns some supervisors' unrealistic expectations that they can be achieved in one self-contained lesson. I have been taught to strive for that and usually I achieve it. But often enough, I must continue a lesson and its aim on another day. Naturally this causes that lesson to occupy part of another period. But one cannot assume variables do not exist: digressions, unanticipated insights, fire drills, PA announcements, discipline problems, latecomers, message interruptions, and other real-life, day-to-day occurrences that never appear in anyone's lesson plan.

Behavioral Objectives

To the best of my recollection, behavioral objectives became an integral part of New York City educators' lesson plans during the early 1980s, when education's critics cried out for ways that both pupils' and teachers' achievements could be more readily measured. The ostensible purpose was to imitate the business "managerial" objective in which an employer could hold an employee accountable.

In the business of education, what such objectives may do is stifle the artistic, although they may also help focus and contain the fledgling. The behavioral objective differs from the aim in that it is stated in such a way to include an observable behavior students will be able to perform after having had the benefit of the classroom lesson. Several concrete examples follow.

1. Pupils will be able to write a paragraph that considers the moral character of Sergeant Waters from Fuller's *A Soldier's Play*.
2. Pupils will be able to defend, in writing, their selections for debate winners on this proposition: that the witches convinced Macbeth to murder Duncan.
3. Pupils will be able to write a paragraph suggesting an alternate conclusion to *Romeo and Juliet*.

4. Pupils will be able to take notes from classmates' oral reports, which summarize characteristics of Ahab, Ishmael, Starbuck, and Queequeg from Melville's *Moby Dick*.

5. Pupils will be able to write a paragraph explaining Hamlet's sighting of the ghost in his mother's room.

6. Pupils will be able to report orally on group discussions involving the following issue: Tom's (from Williams's *The Glass Menagerie*) first responsibility was to further his own life, not support his mother and sister.

7. Pupils will be able to write on the board and copy answers to the following questions: (a) What suggestions does Hawthorne give to show who Pearl's father is? (b) What is your opinion of the townspeople for punishing Hester as they did? (c) What is there about Puritan life in New England that made these people so strict?

8. Pupils will be able to offer oral criticism of Willy Loman's ability to be a father.

9. Pupils will be able to offer oral suggestions on how Mama's $10,000 check *(A Raisin in the Sun)* should have been used.

10. Pupils will be able to define in class, using dictionaries and their homework, at least 10 vocabulary words from the first act of *Hamlet*.

Motivation

Just as in giving a speech or writing a novel, the effective lesson begins with a "hook," or words that will interest the readers and grab their attention from the onset of instruction. This can prove to be very difficult, as Billy Crystal revealed in his portrayal of a professor of English in the film *Throw Mama From the Train* (1987) or Woody Allen's narrative in the beginning of the movie *Manhattan* (1979). Both men introduced their productions by attempting to find and continuing to change the opening line of books they were beginning to write. Thus, while succeeding in making their point about the difficulty of capturing attention, each actor successfully captured his movie audience, particularly any member who ever sought to write an effective opening line!

Gaining the attention of teenagers can be an especially difficult task. When the teacher considers that those adolescents have just made their way into the classroom through corridors dense with people, many arriving with far more pressing problems in their lives than the day's literature lesson, the teacher must be both sensitive and shrewd. A perceptive supervisor once wrote to me, after having observed me teach a lesson on Rolvaag's *Giants in the Earth,* "The opening question, beginning with the phrase, 'If you were a Norwegian . . .,' is essentially irrelevant. Your pupils can no more relate to being a Norwegian than they can to being Flicka." This incisive remark taught me a great deal.

A good motivational introduction to a literature lesson may deal with one or several of the following suggestions:

1. Calling attention to a current event or movie, TV program, or other form of literature that the class shares in common; the event and so forth must be, in some way, analogous to the point of the day's lesson

2. Relating a personal story about your own life or about the life of someone you know; the story should bear a relationship to the lesson's aim

3. Asking the class to interpret a quotation and placing their responses on the board: The quote must be relevant to the lesson's aim

4. Reading an excerpt from a news article relevant to the day's discussion and requesting comment and interpretation

5. Asking one or several pupils to improvise a scene or do a reading relevant to the day's aim

Key to effective motivation is that it is done quickly, begun when the bell rings and completed in no longer than 5 or, at most, 10 minutes. Because the teacher has the legal obligation of taking attendance accurately and of placing assignments on the board, including the aim of the day's lesson, a class, even a reasonably well-disciplined one, might begin to lose interest unless the teacher begins intelligently and promptly. The teacher who begins by taking attendance and doing other procedural tasks before motivating the pupils may find youngsters chatting, passing notes, resting heads on desks, or coming 5 to 10 minutes late to class. "You never get started on time, anyway," they will tell you.

To avoid this, many teachers successfully employ the "Do Now" assignment. This is a task, usually involving writing, placed on the board, that pupils are required to complete during the first 5 minutes of the period. Results may then be used to spur class discussion. Moreover, the writing may be examined for style and structure, and it may be collected, evaluated, and used as a criterion when calculating student grades. The assignment's best feature is that it keeps the youngsters working while routine procedures, even checking homework, can be accomplished. Drawbacks to this assignment include sameness, which turns off more creative pupils. Furthermore, I've observed teachers use more than half a period before the checking, correcting, and discussing of the "Do Now" are completed.

For my own lessons, I begin by placing the homework assignment for the next day on the board. Pupils are expected to copy it immediately. While they do that, I write the aim on another board. If they are still copying, I take attendance. If copying has ceased, I take attendance during one of the lesson's activities. I sign no passes and read no notices before I feel attention to the day's lesson has been gained. This attention I try to gain through one of the aforementioned techniques.

The following are some motivational techniques I've personally used.

1. For a lesson introducing Lawrence's and Lee's *Inherit the Wind:* I'd like to discuss with you today a new religion I've discovered and impress on you that it is a religion that we should all follow. (I wait for objections from pupils.)

2. For a lesson on Macbeth's first soliloquy: How many of you talk to yourselves when completely alone? Why do people do that?

3. For a lesson on Poe's *The Tell-Tale Heart:* Did you ever do anything when you were a child that caused you to feel guilty? What physical feelings did you experience from that?

4. For a lesson on Capek's *RUR* that considers good and evil in humankind: Interpret the following lines taken from Alexander Pope's (1939) *Essay on Man:*

What would this man? Now upward will he soar,
And, little less than angel, would be more (p. 372).

5. For a lesson on Wright's *Native Son* that considers Bigger Thomas's discomfort with Mary Dalton and her boyfriend, Jan: Assume the following—you have taken a job because your mother needs the money to pay for food and rent, and you know you've got to stay out of trouble. The problem is not that the job isn't decent or that the money is bad. The problem is that the employer is of a race or religion that is not the same as yours. In fact, you're the only person of your kind in that place. On the first night of your employment, the boss's daughter or son asks you to pick up her or his boyfriend or girlfriend. Then they ask you, friendly as can be, to take them where you usually hang out with your regular friends. What would you say? What would you do? What feelings would you have?

6. For a lesson on *Romeo and Juliet* or *West Side Story* when the lovers meet for the first time: What is love at first sight? Do you believe in it? In Mario Puzo's (1970) book *The Godfather*, Michael Corleone sees a beautiful girl tending a flock of sheep in the fields of Sicily. He can't take his eyes off her. He is "struck by the thunderbolt," Puzo says (p. 333). Has this ever happened to you? Have you ever, even as a younger child, looked into the face of another and felt you were in love? When? What happened?

7. For a lesson on Buck's *The Good Earth* that considers the role of women in China's society: Who are Margaret Thatcher, Indira Gandhi, Golda Meir, Elizabeth Holtzman, Geraldine Ferraro, Sandra Day O'Connor, and Ruth Bader Ginsberg? Did you know there was a time in America when women did not have the right to vote? What is your opinion about that? What is the women's liberation movement? Do you agree that it is necessary?

8. For a lesson on Wharton's *Ethan Frome* that considers the sanctity of marriage vows: We have reviewed the many reasons people get married, including Ethan's. What are wedding vows? What do they really mean? Let's examine them a little more closely because some of you may one day make them.

9. For a lesson on Rosa Guy's *Friends:* Do you know anyone whom you like but tend to keep your friendship at a minimum with

because something about the person embarrasses you? Or have you ever seen a movie or TV program, or read a book, that shows this kind of feeling? Write briefly why you like the person (real or fictional) but include what the person does that is embarrassing or annoying.

10. For a lesson on Hamlet's inability to avenge his father's murder: Read and interpret the following, taken from *Civilization and Its Discontents* by Freud (1930/1961):

> The element of truth behind all this, which people are so ready to disavow, is that men are not gentle creatures who want to be loved, and who at the most can defend themselves if they are attacked; they are, on the contrary, creatures among whose instinctual endowments is to be reckoned a powerful share of aggressiveness. . . . In consequence of this primary mutual hostility of human beings, civilized society is perpetually threatened with disintegration. (pp. 68-69)

Types of Activities

Teachers of high school English need to remember always that their goal is to improve the communication skills of adolescents. That includes reading, writing, speaking, and listening. In both written and oral work, pupils must demonstrate an ability to apply learning and logic. Clear, rational, supported opinions of an original nature must be elicited by an effective teacher. Elicitation is the technique most acceptable in high schools.

Pivotal Questions

Unlike a university, where professors inculcate pupils with lecture material, high schools use a discovery method based on Socrates's question-answer technique. This has been the traditional activity an English teacher engages in once the motivation is complete. The process is lengthy, but theory suggests that people learn best what they do for themselves.

The teacher must be careful not to ask questions that require merely an affirmative or negative response but to challenge a pupil to offer opinions about why a character behaved a certain way or what one may anticipate a character will do based on prior behavior in the story. By referring a pupil's answer to the rest of the class, the teacher may expect pupils to expand on or contradict peer remarks. The pupils learn more, perhaps, from the process than from the content. They learn to apply logic. They learn to listen.

Good questions actually arise from the lesson's motivation and will be crucial to developing the lesson's aim. Usually only when the aim and motivation are derived can "pivotal" questions, aptly labeled by pedagogues, be phrased. Few in number for a given lesson, these questions are vital to achieving the stated aim and objective of a lesson. Good pivotal questions challenge students to give in-depth responses and use deductive reasoning. Students should be offered facts and opinions from which they may draw generalizations. This is the nature of the pivotal question. In addition, such questions are usually best begun with the following words: *describe, explain, why, how, evaluate,* and so forth. Some sample pivotal questions follow:

1. Describe the Younger household from Hansbury's *A Raisin in the Sun*.
2. Why does Hemingway show Santiago, from *The Old Man and the Sea*, climbing the mountain with a mast on his shoulder?
3. Why does Atticus Finch decide to defend Tom Robinson?
4. Explain why you feel proud of Kumalo from Paton's *Cry, the Beloved Country*.
5. Explain Brutus's reasoning for joining the conspiracy against Caesar.
6. Evaluate Joe's decision to protect his family business (from Miller's *All My Sons*).
7. How did Chillingworth taunt Dimmesdale in Hawthorne's *The Scarlet Letter*?
8. Describe and explain Smirnov's mood as he enters Popov's home in Chekhov's *The Boor*.
9. Describe Jane's feelings when she first meets Mr. Rochester in Brontë's *Jane Eyre*.
10. Evaluate Hamlet's choice of Fortinbras to rule Denmark.

During my tenure as a teacher of communication skills, my one-time principal, Dr. Jack M. Pollock, a former teacher and supervisor of English, once distributed to the English department a memo that enumerated the qualities of good questioning technique. A partial list of these qualities pertaining only to the planning stages of lessons follows.

1. Thought-provoking questions (Why? How?) are preferable to straight fact questions, though some "What?" questions may have to be asked to get the necessary facts on which thinking is based.

2. The best type of developmental lesson is based on three or four pivotal questions that will provoke lively discussion from the class, with occasional challenges from the teacher that centralize the lesson. On these pivotal questions you may hang the facts and events of the novel, biography, or play you are discussing. (The use of the broad, thought- and discussion-provoking pivotal question is not always possible, especially with unresponsive, apathetic classes, but it should be kept in mind as an ideal. In such classes and in all lower-term classes, discussion should not go on beyond half the period. Other activities, such as boardwork, vocabulary, dramatization, and further reading should be planned. Your aim is maximum student activity and expression, not teacher activity and lecture.)

3. Keep the aim of your lesson in mind when planning questions. Each should be related to the whole purpose: Avoid mere "covering ground." (Again, this is not always possible, particularly when you're teaching a long novel and assigning a few chapters every night.) Before planning the lesson or listing pivotal questions, decide what you want your pupils to get out of this.

4. Try to draw from the literary selections that which will appeal to pupils' present interests and that will be meaningful in terms of the lives they are now living.

5. When possible, draw on the past knowledge of the pupils. When teaching a book, ask pupils to make comparisons of aspects of it to aspects of another piece of literature they've studied together.

6. The aim of questioning is not merely to get information but also to cultivate oral expression. Questions should call for some discussion, not merely one-word answers. Allow several pupils to participate in the discussion provoked by any one question. Correct errors in grammar and pronunciation but do so casually and quickly without interrupting the trend of the lesson.

7. Lessons should have unity. One question should grow logically out of another and come to a definite conclusion.

8. Questions should not be
   a. Alternative (Does the Nile River flow toward the north or south?)
   b. Categorical (Was John Adams the second president of the United States?)
   c. Leading (Should the blood be drawn to the brain when it is needed in the stomach?)
   d. Elliptical (The capital of New York City is . . .)

9. Questions should be
   a. Clear (Avoid difficult vocabulary and phrasing.)
   b. Pointed (Avoid "How was the Battle of Gettysburg fought?" Pupils will miss the question's aim.)
   c. Single (Avoid two or three questions twisted into one requiring diverse answers.)

Other Activities

In developing a plan to teach literature, it is vital to include activities that encourage widespread student participation. Equally important is including activities that help determine whether pupils are, in fact, reading and writing the prescribed assignments. One method is to provide brief quizzes at the beginning of a lesson. Questions on such quizzes may be of the type that demand simple, one-word answers yet serve as a check that material has been at least read, if not analyzed. Another method involves having pupils recite all or part of their homework during the lesson.

Boardwork by pupils is another activity that helps determine whether they have done their homework. Responses to in-class questions or to homework assignments may be written on the board by several pupils, while a separate oral activity is concomitantly pursued.

Boardwork and Note Taking

Boardwork is crucial to a good lesson. My experience has taught me that high school students, with few exceptions, look forward to maintaining a record in their notebooks of the material covered while a lesson is in session. Therefore, it becomes incumbent on the teacher to prepare materials that will be placed on the board either by the pupils or the teacher during the actual lesson.

Good boardwork is, without debate, a vital component to an exemplary lesson. First, it provides an opportunity for practice in writing skills, especially when the pupils are writing on the board. Second, it gives pupils a sense of gratification when they see their words and ideas as the center of attention on the board. Third, it provides pupils with a working activity rather than the more passive one of listening. Finally, it supplies material from which to study. After all, how do pupils studying not only literature but also math, science, social studies, and a foreign language remember what was taught in a lesson about Richard Wright's *Black Boy* if they have no permanent record of the lesson in class?

My preference for boardwork involves a "power" question dealing directly with the lesson's aim. For example, if a lesson's aim is, "How do conditions in the Hunsdorfer home (from Zindel's *The Effect of Gamma Rays on Man-in-the-Moon Marigolds*) suggest a bad environment for a growing child?" we might elicit the following list from the pupils on the conditions that exist in that home. The boardwork might look like this:

Conditions in the Hunsdorfer Home

1. Curtains are faded.
2. Newspapers, magazines, and dishes are scattered about.
3. Wire cage is on a table.
4. Kitchen window is covered with newspapers.
5. Ugly drapes line the windows.

6. Mother is a hypocrite—she lies to the teacher and is sarcastic to her children (Pupils might argue that this is not a "condition" similar to the first five).

An obvious follow-up question should take into account pupils' opinions of such environmental conditions and how they might be improved. Answers to this question may be recorded on the board along with final responses to the lesson's aim.

Another technique of using boardwork is to ask several pupils to write their homework answers on the board while the teacher develops the lesson or checks other pupils' homework in another way. At the appropriate time, each homework answer written on the board may be reviewed and discussed. Grammatical corrections may be supplied and additions or subtractions may be made to the answers by other pupils, who may then also write on the board. Pupils may copy such notes into their notebooks or construct notes with their own meanings and interpretations. Praise should be liberally offered to all who write on the board.

Although boardwork is vital, it should not consume an entire period. Asking students to copy notes *ad infinitum* from the board is unwieldy, boring busywork. I have also observed that asking pupils to place lengthy answers on the board often wastes time because they simply take too long in writing.

Silent Reading

Usually silent reading is regarded as busywork (work assigned merely to keep the pupils occupied, with no other educational intent). Silent reading can, however, be a practical activity when correctly applied. For example, the teacher has spent a period motivating the reading of Poe's *The Tell-Tale Heart*. The last several minutes may be wisely devoted to letting the pupils actually get into the text while they remain eager (from the lesson) for it.

Another suggestion for useful silent reading involves incorporating it with a question such as, "Which lines in the soliloquy seem to imply that Hamlet is suicidal?" One might cogently argue, however, that such an assignment is more suitable for homework, except that in class the discussion might be better guided, especially given the difficulty of Shakespearean language. The point is that silent reading should nearly always be accompanied by a question demanding thinking, writing, speaking, or listening. Silent reading must not exist in a purposeless vacuum, suggesting that the teacher is uncreative and dull.

Oral Reading

Perhaps a more palatable activity during a literature lesson includes calling on students to read aloud. This gives the instructor opportunities to work on oral components of communication, such as volume, rate, phrasing, pronunciation, emotion, and so forth. Moreover, the teacher may find occasion for giving praise, thus encouraging and achieving greater pupil confidence. In addition, pupils required to respond to such performances are expected to listen to their peers read. Pupils should be called on to read scenes from plays, verses from poetry, excerpts from novels, short stories, essays, and homework or assigned original writing based on the day's literary discussion.

The portions teachers choose to have read aloud need to be selected with care. They must, in some way, help to achieve the lesson's aim. For example, if the aim asks, "What effect does Jim's visit have on Laura in Williams's *The Glass Menagerie?*" a portion of the scene during which the couple meets, converses, and dances would seem a logical choice to read aloud. In fact, the pupils might even be asked to "stage" the scene in front of the class. But merely reading the scene without comment or analysis is a wasted effort. The teacher must not forget that part of the purpose of reading a scene or excerpt aloud is to encourage analysis. Therefore, strategic pauses for questions must be incorporated into such lessons. For example, a pupil may be asked to reread a line and the class asked, "Why did Laura react that way?" or "What emotions are behind Laura's words when she says, '. . .' ?"

The teacher can also use the opportunity to evoke emotional delivery from readers, calling on some pupils to explain the feelings of characters and encouraging readers to reread lines, adding the appropriate vocal and physical reactions. Results sometimes provide surprisingly improved recitation.

Care must be taken by the teacher to avoid insisting that the painfully shy read aloud or that pupils who read very poorly be called on to play major roles. Problems arise in such cases, not merely for the performer but also for the listening audience. Oral reading should be an occasion to stimulate interest in the literature, not stamp it out. To that end it is sometimes wise for the teacher to read aloud especially difficult passages, interjecting, of course, questions that provoke thinking, critical analysis, and oral response. Shakespearean lines in bulk, for example, are usually better handled by the teacher, at least until pupils begin to appreciate the language, vocabulary, and flow of the poetic rhythms.

Oral poetry reading has similar aims to oral drama. But in addition, the teacher can use the opportunity to ask pupils to read lines in unison and call forth individual feelings in lines. Although perhaps somewhat outdated as a technique, choral reading may enable those who do not read aloud well—or do not volunteer—to become willing and successful participants in class, thus providing a good way to bolster their confidence. Certain poems lend themselves to, for example, the higher-pitched sound of a female voice, whereas others may call for the lower-pitched sounds made by the male larynx. James Weldon Johnson's *The Creation* and Poe's *The Bells* are superb examples of poetry easily adapted to this method.

Another technique of oral reading, often useful for prose, including novels, biographies, short stories, and essays, is to ask a question that necessitates the use of passages from the text to answer. Too much silent reading is time-consuming and the teacher should require that only the page or two on which the needed passage lies be perused. For example, pupils may be asked to read a few pages to locate how Edith Wharton magnifies Ethan Frome's feelings of guilt before his evening alone with Mattie.

In any case, reading aloud must never be an end in itself. Reading aloud should be used as a way to help achieve the aim of the lesson, to provide variety and increase interest in the class, and most important, to help students improve all communication skills, thinking included. The oral reading must not exist in a vacuum but must be accompanied by questions demanding analytical consideration.

Debate

Debates in class may be highly stylized and formal, in the tradition of college tournaments. On the other hand, they may merely involve discussing an issue arising from the literature on which the teacher expected controversy or on which students focused because it seemed important to them. In any case, debate is a marvelous device to employ because it brings so many communication skills to the fore. Debate calls for a class not merely to read text but to scrutinize it. Debate demands that pupils prepare notes, including arguments and counterarguments, and requires clear speaking and intense listening.

Some propositions taken from literature that make excellent long-range assignments and take an entire period (or more) to complete follow:

1. That Lady Macbeth convinced Macbeth to kill Duncan
2. That Atticus Finch should not have taken Tom Robinson's case
3. That Hamlet was not a procrastinator
4. That Lena Younger should not have given any money to Walter
5. That Ethan Frome should have run away with Mattie
6. That Bigger Thomas should not have been executed
7. That *Death of a Salesman* is successful modern tragedy in the classical sense
8. That Tom Wingfield should not have left his mother and sister
9. That Moby Dick is a symbol of evil
10. That Nora Helmer was right to leave her husband and children

A long-range debate assignment can fill a complete lesson, during which time the class should be nearly 100% self-sufficient. Obviously, lessons on debate rules and format must be taught prior to the actual debate. The breakdown of the traditional 40-minute lesson for a self-contained debate may be handled as follows:

1. Constructive speeches (12 minutes)
   a. 1st affirmative (3 minutes)

      b. 1st negative (3 minutes)
      c. 2nd affirmative (3 minutes)
      d. 2nd negative (3 minutes)
  2. Team conference (5 minutes)
  3. Rebuttal speeches (8 minutes)
      a. 1st negative (2 minutes)
      b. 1st affirmative (2 minutes)
      c. 2nd negative (2 minutes)
      d. 2nd affirmative (2 minutes)
  4. Judging (5 minutes)

Pupils not involved in the speaking part of the debate are required to complete a debate ballot, usually a checklist indicating reactions to the debaters' arguments, including reasoning, organization, research, and delivery. The bottom of the ballot should contain a statement similar to, "The best debating was done by the _____ team because _____." The first blank space is to be filled in with either "affirmative" or "negative." The second blank space must be completed with a reason for the choice. The teacher or a pupil (perhaps the timekeeper) then collects the ballots and tallies them. Ballots without reasons for choices are discarded. A winner is announced. This procedure usually takes 5 to 10 minutes. The remainder of the period (if any) may be devoted to the following simple question: "What did you learn this period about the literature and the issue debated?"

A debate in the classroom need not, however, be such a formidable experience. The debate can occupy only a part of a period during which an issue arises and pupils take positions. Some examples follow.

1. That Lady Macbeth's faint was faked
2. That Absalom Kumalo deserved execution
3. That Romeo could have avoided the fight with Tybalt
4. That Captain and Mrs. Keller mistreated Helen
5. That Biff and Happy are immature characters
6. That Phyllisia (from Guy's *Friends*) is a snob
7. That Brady is the greatest character in *Inherit the Wind*
8. That Eliza Doolittle is a stupid young girl

9. That Tess should have revealed the truth to Angel
10. That Sidney Carton should not have sacrificed his life

These issues seem of lesser magnitude than the preceding 10 propositions suggested for more formalized debate. They are, therefore, easier to include in a briefer time within one period. The teacher may place the question on the board with columns for affirmative and negative responses. The proposition, in fact, need not be formal and might be better served when phrased in question form with "yes" and "no" columns on the board.

IS PHYLLISIA A SNOB?

Yes   No

Under each column go reasons pupils offer for their stances. The teacher should, when preparing, devise both affirmative and negative responses to encourage thinking and participation during the activity. This particular activity might take between 15 and 20 minutes, after which a summary and second activity should be used. The logical conclusion of such a lesson might require eliciting pupil opinions of the issue based on the reasoning done during class.

Original Writing

Requiring pupils to write on a daily basis to improve both their logic and style has been a goal of theorists of English pedagogy for many years. Although I have found that such exercises may improve thinking skills and may even improve a pupil's desire to write, they do not improve fundamental writing skills unless the teacher edits and corrects each pupil's papers, classwork and homework included. This, of course, is next to impossible. The typical teacher of English in a modern public urban high school may have as many as 150 adolescents attending class with regularity. There is simply not enough time to correct all this original work. Still, teachers are always encouraged to assign it and check it in some way. In my opinion a great deal of writing should be done by students and evaluated by teachers so noticeable improvement in the skill will occur.

The dilemma cannot resolve itself well. Yes, assignments may be given, but evaluations tend to exist in the form of spot checks merely to see if the work has been completed rather than to improve its quality. There are, however, some useful techniques that teachers use for the evaluation of original writing:

1. Specific composition and book report work must, of course, be thoroughly corrected and evaluated.
2. If a teacher has five classes, four sets of homework or class-work are merely checked and one thoroughly corrected and evaluated.
3. Spot checks and evaluations are done briefly during class.
4. Several pupils' work in each class is collected on an arbitrary basis, corrected and evaluated.

The business of evaluation is, however, tangential to the matter at hand, which is the use of original writing as an activity during a literature lesson. Such writing may occur at any point during the lesson, when the teacher asks pupils to respond to a question by placing pen to paper. Even the opening motivational device might require a written response:

1. Write about the first time you were physically attracted to someone and you felt that you were in love.
2. Select a TV program you watch and describe one of its episodes that caused you to cry.
3. Have you ever been in a situation that made you feel different from everyone else? What happened? Discuss it in 75 to 100 words.
4. The teacher might read an article, relate an example, ask several pupils to read or improvise a scene, and then require the class to react to it in writing.
5. Write what you remember about yesterday's literature discussion.

The teacher may circulate about the room at this point and offer corrections and suggestions for individual papers. Care should be taken not to allow pupils to take too long in writing. No more than

7 or 8 minutes should be allocated for daily writing of this nature. Once completed, pupils may read their answers or use them as notes from which to extemporize. I do not admonish pupils who are unable to produce writing during such an assignment. They must, however, make an earnest attempt at thinking. Eventually, some or all of this writing, at the teacher's discretion, may be collected. On occasion students may be called on to share papers with one another for peer evaluation.

During the lesson, either after the motivation or any time before the conclusion, the teacher may pose a question demanding a written response. Several examples follow:

1. What mood has Melville established in his first several paragraphs of *Moby Dick?* Point out specific words and phrases that help create that mood.
2. What effects did prairie life have on Beret?
3. Should Satan, from *Paradise Lost,* be described as physically ugly or physically beautiful? Explain.
4. Write your reaction to Gene's pushing Finney out of the tree.
5. How can you tell, from Sergius's behavior and Louka's words, that Shaw does not believe in the "higher love"?
6. Discuss the obvious differences between Chanticleer and Pertilotte.
7. Why does Anita decide to help Maria even after she knows Tony killed Bernardo? Would you have helped her? Explain.
8. Evaluate Beatrice's treatment of Nanny. What would you advise her to do?
9. Discuss then reasons Willy Loman is not in a good mood as the play opens.
10. Discuss your feelings toward Cordelia for the way she expressed her love for her father.

Possibly the best moment to acquire original writing is near the lesson's conclusion, when the teacher may attempt to achieve the aim and objective. There are some very simple ways of handling this aspect of assigning original writing. The first is requiring the pupils to maintain a daily journal in which they record reactions to and descriptions of each lesson. This is a more than reasonable routine that establishes good work habits and probably helps pupils to write more and, perhaps, better. This is not, however, my favorite way of producing original writing. First, it tends to be dull by its own routine nature. I can imagine hearing many audible sighs of disgust at the direction, "Take out your journal." Second, the journal entry may not necessarily cover the teacher's aim and objective for the lesson.

In lieu of the journal assignment, the teacher might occasionally (to avoid the tedium of routine) ask the pupils, as the end of the lesson draws near, to record what they learned during the period. But in my opinion, best of all is to ask a question that guides the pupils to answers that fulfill the outcomes the teacher seeks:

1. Based on the conclusion to Act I, what do you predict for the Loman family in Act II?
2. What is your opinion of Chris for telling his father about Larry's death?
3. What is your opinion of John Proctor for withholding his confession?
4. In what ways did Nora show she was, at the very least, Helmer's emotional equal?
5. Based on reports from Wilkie and Peterson, what feelings have you developed for Sergeant Waters?
6. Discuss Claudius's intelligence, based on his behavior and circumstances in Act I, Scene 2.
7. What should Mama Younger have done with the $10,000? How can you tell?
8. What do you believe will happen to Wang Lung's land after he dies? How can you tell?
9. What attempts did Morrison make to soften your feelings about Charley?

If enough time is provided, pupils may be called on to read their answers aloud and to respond to one another in kind.

Original writing, other than the daily type (brief and pointed), may be of a lengthier nature. Examinations, when given, should nearly always afford pupils the opportunity of expressing themselves at length in writing. In addition, compositions based on literature may be assigned. Examples are to be found in the Resources.

Improvisation

One or several pupils may be called on to enact a scenario prepared by the teacher, which may be used as a motivation or as an activity for discussion. Pupils may be asked to perform any of the following:

1. Imagine you will be left without an English teacher for the term. Assume that no adult will arrive to assist you and that you will be totally alone. Still, your graduation is pending. Several of you are asked to "step out" of the situation and observe. After 5 minutes the teacher assumes normal duties again. (Improvisation for Golding's *Lord of the Flies*)
2. Your boyfriend or girlfriend, whom you love dearly and trust implicitly, reveals to you that he or she wants to commit a serious and illegal action to attain something, for example, a job that will earn him or her a great deal of money and respect. Discuss the situation together. (Improvisation for *Macbeth*)
3. Your roommate or best friend is about to go out with a girl or boy you truly feel is special. All your friend seems interested in is sex. (Improvisation for Salinger's *Catcher in the Rye*)
4. You observe a big boy or girl constantly picking on a smaller boy or girl because the bigger one doesn't like the fact that the little one knows so many answers in class. You stick up for the smaller boy or girl. (Improvisation for Guy's *The Friends*)
5. You're with a group of your friends who keep belittling a new boy or girl in the neighborhood. You think this new person is OK, but you are reluctant to argue with your friends. (Improvisation for Rose's *Twelve Angry Men*)
6. You break up with your boyfriend or girlfriend and return all his or her gifts and love letters— and you offer no reason to explain your change of attitude because you can't say that your father is forcing you to do this. You really still love the boy or girl. (Improvisation for *Hamlet*)
7. You've fallen in love with your cousin's boyfriend or girlfriend. Your cousin treats him or her very badly and he or she has been noticeably unhappy for a long time. He or she

finally tells you he or she cares for you. (Improvisation for Wharton's *Ethan Frome*)

8. You and a couple of your friends have no way to get money, so you discuss robbing a local grocery store. You're the one who's most scared about doing it. (Improvisation for Wright's *Native Son*)

9. You are two brothers or sisters talking about old times and the decline you've noticed in your father's mental abilities. (Improvisation for Miller's *Death of a Salesman*)

10. You talk with members of your gang about the hatred you share for a rival gang in the neighborhood. (Improvisation for Laurents's *West Side Story*)

The material for the improvisations may be drawn from experiences teenagers have had, may have, may know from friends' experiences, or have shared vicariously through some form of the media. Analogies may be made from the improvisation to the literature at hand, which can lead to fruitful discussion. As a classroom activity, improvisation is not limited to teen experiences, although it might be naive to ask pupils to imagine they are Macbeth and Lady Macbeth, though less unrealistic to ask them to feel what Romeo and Juliet felt on first seeing each other.

Performance (Memorized)

I recall my English teacher in my senior year of high school assigning Macbeth's "Tomorrow and tomorrow and tomorrow" soliloquy to the entire class for memorization and performance. After approximately a week or two, he used several class periods to require students to recite the monologue, and I was nervously among them. I no longer remember how those performance lessons were taught, but I still know the soliloquy by heart. Moreover, on meeting people later in life, more than several have recalled similar assignments from high school, the results of which, among other things, left lines of poetry or prose forever imprinted on their memories and appreciated in their hearts. This does not mean, of course, that there aren't those who look back with distaste on those days of recitation and have done what they can to repress memories of those anxiety-laden days.

Despite some obvious benefits, I have never used this technique in my English classes, other than in electives in drama or acting, because I believe the nervousness factor detracts too much from real enjoyment of the literature. Furthermore, unless the teacher of English is specially trained in oral interpretation, many performances may be articulated without understanding. Finally, it takes at least two class periods to hear and critique over 30 performances of the same monologue—tedious in itself. Several readings of the same lines on the day they are relevant to the teacher's aim seem more appropriate. One way to decrease the tedium of multiple performances is to allow pupils to select one of several monologues from a play. This also allows a pupil to study the most personally satisfying monologue.

Although I personally do not like the aforementioned memorization activity, I do recognize its merit and suggest its use to add variety to the teaching of poetry and dramatic literature.

Symposium

Because of the nature of the symposium[1], which incorporates preparation of individual speeches on a given subject, this assignment is recommended for long-range study. The teacher certainly needs time to explain the meaning and methods used in delivering a symposium and then break the class into groups to prepare and divide the responsibility. Several weeks' time should be allowed for preparation and research and a full period allowed for each group to perform its symposium. A symposium lesson generally follows a specific format. A group member places the research question on the board along with a list of speakers. One group member takes the role of moderator and introduces each speaker and topic. Each speaker (minimum of five to maximum of eight) delivers his or her materials while the class takes pertinent notes. When all speakers have concluded, the moderator (who also makes a speech) asks the class to address questions to members of the group, who sit in front of the room. The following list suggests subjects for symposium:

1. Each group is assigned a short story writer. Each member of the group is assigned to report on the elements of one short story

by that writer. The same assignment works well for a specific
novelist, playwright, or poet.

2. Each group is assigned an issue traditionally discussed in
   Hamlet: (a) Hamlet's sanity, (b) the women in *Hamlet*, (c)
   Hamlet's procrastination, (d) imagery in *Hamlet*, (e) Hamlet's
   soliloquies.

3. Each group is assigned an aspect of Chinese culture in conjunction with a study of Buck's *The Good Earth:* (a) family structure, (b) climate and geography, (c) leadership and politics,
   (d) religion and superstition, (e) economics. This assignment
   may be used for other books about foreign cultures, such as
   Markandaya's *Nectar in a Sieve,* Paton's *Cry, the Beloved Country,*
   Wilde's *The Importance of Being Earnest,* Solzhenitsyn's *One
   Day in the Life of Ivan Denisovitch,* and so forth. This assignment
   can be applied to nearly any literary piece that is a product of a
   particular place, time period, and so forth; for example, Miller's
   The Crucible, All My Sons, and *Death of a Salesman;* Hemingway's
   A Farewell to Arms and *For Whom the Bell Tolls;* Steinbeck's *The
   Grapes of Wrath;* Wright's *Native Son;* Hawthorne's *The Scarlet
   Letter;* Crane's *The Red Badge of Courage;* Chekhov's *The Cherry
   Orchard;* and many, many more.

4. Each group is assigned a component of literature for analysis,
   for example, plot structure, thematic elements, stylistic devices,
   symbolism, characters, and so forth.

The symposium lesson needs ample time allotted for pupil questions and a critique session that evokes content-oriented discussion
and comments designed to improve organization and the delivery of
speeches. Note taking should be part of the experience also; speakers
can be required to write on the board and audience members can be
required to take notes and summarize, in writing, each speaker's
presentation.

Oral Book Report

A good activity for teaching poise, confidence, speaking technique, and literature is the oral book report. A general question or a choice
of questions may be posed to pupils, who are then given approxi-

mately 3 weeks to 1 month to read and prepare to extemporize on the book. I have learned that an important component to every question is the requirement that each pupil quote from the text two or three times during the performance. The time limit should be 4 to 5 minutes. Several useful suggestions follow.

1. Female characters in literature are often stereotyped into roles expected of them by the society in which they live. From the book you read, choose a female character and show that she is a stereotypical character or that she is an atypical one.

2. Good literature generally involves a plot that is memorable because of some outstanding moments. From the book you read, select several outstanding moments and explain how they helped make the book interesting.

3. A good writer sometimes makes a book seem like real life because of the dialogue. Select several examples of the dialogue from the book you read and discuss their importance in making the literature seem true to life.

4. Heroism is not always exhibited by slaying a dragon or jumping into a burning building. Often people are heroes for committing small, sometimes unnoticed acts of bravery. From the book you read, select a character and discuss his or her bravery.

5. Relationships are often ruined because people do not communicate well together. From the book you read, choose two people who have a poor relationship and discuss both where their problems in communication lie and how they might be able to alleviate these problems.

6. Books are filled with their writers' ideas about life. Choose one of the writer's ideas from the book you read and show how the writer made that idea clear through the plot and the character.

7. Where a story is set helps to create mood for the reader. From the book you read, discuss the setting(s) in which the story takes place, showing how those places affect the characters and set a mood for the reader.

8. Characters in books nearly always have to overcome obstacles to survive. From the book you read, choose a character and

discuss how he or she overcame or failed to overcome obstacles in his or her life.

For oral book reports to be successful, prior lessons on speaking technique should be taught, including principles dealing with the relevance and use of quoted material, techniques of introduction and conclusion, outlining, vocal expression and audibility, eye contact, and more. The actual book report lesson incorporates approximately five reports, with encouraging feedback offered from both pupils and teacher after each one. The teacher should offer each pupil who speaks, a written evaluation of his or her performance, and audience members should be required to comment in writing on each report. In a class of 30+ pupils, therefore, about six or seven periods of 40 minutes each are necessary to complete all reports. The pupils in the audience may be asked each report day to select their favorite report of the day and offer reasons for their choice, to gain practice in original writing.

Panel Discussion

Panel discussion[2] is a group effort that is considerably different in technique from the symposium. Although each member is expected to be an expert in the group's assigned subject, members must follow, either loosely or closely, an outlined series of steps to explore and investigate a literary question. Comments and speaker order remain spontaneous throughout the performance. The following outline presents John Dewey's Steps of Reflective Thinking (McBurney & Hance, 1950, pp. 65-83):

    I. Recognition of the Problem
        A. Phrasing the problem as a question
        B. Defining the problem
   II. Analysis of the Problem
        A. History of the problem
        B. Effects of the problem
        C. Causes of the problem
        D. Criteria by which to suggest solutions
  III. Suggestion of Solutions

IV. Evaluation of Solutions
V. Choice of Best Solution

Groups may be given a literary question to study and research that involves both critical thinking and evaluation. A full period may be devoted to a panel's presentation; the next day, questions may be posed and feedback on the discussion and communication technique may be offered by the audience and teacher. Discussion questions are best derived by the group itself, but that is a time-consuming procedure. Several examples of questions for this activity follow.

1. Does Miller's *Death of a Salesman* succeed as modern, Aristotelian tragedy?
2. How is Puritanism reflected in the thinking of the major characters in Hawthorne's *The Scarlet Letter?*
3. Who are the protagonists and antagonists in Williams's *A Streetcar Named Desire?*
4. What is the significance of the white whale in Melville's *Moby Dick?*
5. Is Bigger Thomas a sympathetic character in Wright's *Native Son?*
6. Should the language in Shakespeare's work be updated and Americanized for today's American high school students to study?
7. How is Malamud's *The Assistant* affected by the era and society about which it is written?
8. Are the graphic sexual passages necessary to the effectiveness of Morrison's *The Bluest Eye?*
9. Is Wilder's *Our Town* still effective drama as we approach the 21st century?
10. Is Wilson's *The Piano Lesson* effective in delivering its message about black heritage?

Collaborative Learning

Some time in the late 1970s or early 1980s it was discovered that placing youngsters in groups—not only in English but in all classes—would produce greater class participation. It was also believed that this method would raise students' level of learning, personal responsibility, and ability to communicate. I do not doubt the wisdom of the observations and research done in this area, especially when considering the effects I have achieved in my own classrooms using this form of instruction. I remain, however, well aware that difficulties exist in the execution of collaborative learning. For example, despite all best intentions, participation is never equal. Some group members dominate, whereas others withdraw. Some are frequently absent. Others are lazy or lack concentration. In addition, by diluting individual responsibility, group work of this nature allows lazy people to "hide" and is not challenging enough for more diligent pupils. In general, when groups do poorly it is because of personality clashes between members. Although the teacher's role in such an endeavor is reduced to that of a facilitator in the classroom, the part the teacher must play remains vital in both preparation and presentation. Literature on collaborative learning exists in abundance and can be of aid while dealing with the pitfalls of the process.

During preparation, the teacher must be sure to create challenging situations and questions for each group. These groups should be formed, in my opinion, not at random but based on pupils' individual differences. I have observed that homogeneous groups do not succeed as well as heterogeneous, probably because the lack of balance produces one-way thinking. All pupils in a group should not be of the same sex, religion, race, or personality type when that can be avoided. A group entirely of quiet people might be too dull. A group entirely of aggressive people could prove too quarrelsome.

Instruction to pupils about to embark on a collaborative learning adventure must be properly administered, especially with regard to individual roles during participation in group session, selection and rotation of group spokespeople and recorders, time limits, returning attention to the center of the class for note taking, acceptable behavior while other groups perform, and forming conclusions. Facilitation of each lesson must be sharp and thorough to avoid one lesson running into another. The teacher's role should include the following:

1. Placing the aim on the board
2. Distributing the day's assignments

3. Circulating about the room and assisting groups as needed (asking extending questions and coaching students are teacher tasks critical to the success of group learning)
4. Coordinating questions from members of other groups to performing groups
5. Ensuring pupils are taking notes
6. Adding or correcting information; eliciting additions or corrections from pupils
7. Asking questions involving original writing
8. Supplying transitional material
9. Eliciting conclusions and achievement of objective
10. Assigning homework for the period

A good collaborative learning lesson incorporates all the essentials of the traditional lesson. The lesson should, if properly timed (poor timing is one of its serious shortcomings), be self-contained and pupil-dominated during both in-class preparation and performance of assignments. Assignments should meet most if not all of the following criteria:

1. Material challenging pupils' age and skills level
2. Previous night's reading and homework incorporated
3. Reading material used in deriving answers
4. Ideas shared
5. Enough material provided to produce participation from all group members
6. Materials relevant and significant to aim of lesson

Examples of collaborative learning lessons appear in the Resources.

Medial Summary and Transition

In the traditional lesson involving teacher-directed activities, usually question-answer periods, some type of summation is helpful in the middle of the session to remind the pupils of the lesson's purpose and to review any conclusions reached by that point. Moreover, the teacher might also use the moment to link what has been achieved at that point to what the remainder of the lesson will contain. A number of examples follow.

1. In a lesson on *Romeo and Juliet* in which the aim is, "Why do Romeo and Juliet fall in love during their first meeting?" and the first activity is a group session dealing with the issue of love at first sight and why it happens to people, the medial summary might include listing on the board ideas formulated by each group. The transition might be, "Now that we've considered some reasons why people fall in love at first sight, let's examine Shakespeare's text and see what happens to Romeo and Juliet."

2. In a lesson on Miller's *Death of a Salesman* in which the aim is, "To what extent was Biff affected by the incident in Boston?" and the first activity involves reading aloud the scene in which Biff discovers Willy with another woman, the medial summary might be to elicit from pupils and list on the board Biff's immediate emotions and their causes. A transition could be, "Now that we've observed Biff's trauma, let's examine how it affected various parts of his life."

3. In a lesson on *The Autobiography of Malcolm X* in which the aim is, "What did Malcolm learn in Mecca?" and the first activity involves a question-answer session and listing on the board the various Islamic traditions Malcolm observed, the medial summary could be to write a statement on the board from pupils suggesting Malcolm's overall impression of Mecca. The transition could be, "Now that we've examined Malcolm's observations and impressions of Mecca, let's determine what new philosophies he developed from them."

4. In a lesson on Wharton's *Ethan Frome* in which the aim is, "What does the author do to heighten tension the day of the evening that Ethan and Mattie are to be alone?" and the first activity involves a discussion of feelings people have when they are thinking about or planning something unethical, the medial summary might include listing on the board several experiences people have had while they were in the midst of thinking about or planning something unethical. The transition could be, "Now that we understand the causes of these feelings, let's see how well Edith Wharton understood them and captured them in her book."

5. In a lesson on Paton's *Cry, the Beloved Country* in which the aim is, "What hope does Paton give readers regarding the disintegration of apartheid in South Africa?" and the first activity involves eliciting textual evidence and listing on the board the visible effects of apartheid, the medial summary might include eliciting a statement from pupils regarding the ultimate result (destructive, bloody war) of apartheid. The transition could be, "Now that we've seen the ugliness of apartheid, has Alan Paton given his readers any hope of improvement in his book?"

6. In a lesson on *Macbeth* in which the aim is, "How does Shakespeare use visual imagery to enhance the nightmarelike atmosphere in Act II?" and the first activity involves explaining visual imagery and observing it in Act II, Scene 1, the medial summary might include defining visual imagery and writing two examples from Act II, Scene 1 on the board. The transition could be, "Now that we understand the meaning of visual imagery, let's examine where and why Shakespeare uses it in the rest of Act II."

7. In a lesson on Hansbury's *A Raisin in the Sun* in which the aim is, "Was it a good decision for Mama to give Walter the $6,500?" and the first activity involves locating the evidence from the text on which Mama based her decision to give Walter the money, the medial summary might include listing on the board Mama's reasons for giving Walter the money. The transition could be, "Now that we know Mama's reasons, do you believe she made the right decision?"

8. In a lesson on Wilder's *Our Town* in which the aim is, "What do George and Emily learn about each other in Act II?" and the first activity involves an oral reading of George and Emily's awkward scene together, the medial summary might include writing an elicited list of reasons on the board for why George and Emily felt awkward. The transition could be, "Now that we understand why George and Emily feel awkward, let's examine what they are learning about each other and why."

9. In a lesson on Lawrence and Lee's *Inherit the Wind* in which the aim is, "Whose entrance into Hillsboro is more dramatic, Brady's or Drummond's?" and the first activity involves an oral reading of Brady's entrance to Hillsboro, the medial summary might include asking pupils first to write and then to read their impressions of

Brady's entrance to Hillsboro. The transition could be, "Now that we've examined Brady's entrance, let's study Drummond's entrance and then compare the two."

Although I have seen many successful lessons without medial summaries and have taught more lessons than not without medial summaries, it should be made clear to any teacher that the medial summary is, nonetheless, an important step in a developmental lesson. The medial summary keeps both pupils and teacher focused, thereby increasing the possibility of learning taking place.

The Second Activity

Once past the too-often-forgotten medial summary, teachers need to consider a second activity as they progress toward achieving the session's aim. Although we no longer need a lengthy explanation of the types of activities, because they have already been discussed, the teacher should be advised at this juncture that another activity must be undertaken and that the lesson is far from over.

The second activity may involve further oral reading, if that's how the lesson began, or further group work, if that's how the lesson began. The second activity, of course, may differ from the first. If the first activity involved discussion and note taking, the second might call for silent reading, reading aloud the homework previously assigned, original writing, and so forth. Individual lessons might prove successful with one constant activity or with a variety of activities. Some good advice is not to use the same activity every day, for example, "OK. Open your books to page 52, where we left off yesterday."

Achieving the Aim and Objective

If a lesson is taught "right," a teacher is supposed to have some measurable way to judge if the aim has been achieved and what or whether the pupils have learned. This is, in my opinion, questionable theory. Pupils may be capable of writing or speaking a response to a question such as, "Why did Ricky Braithwaite (*To Sir, With Love*) decide to continue teaching at Greenslade despite overbearing pressure?" without fully understanding the lesson's aim, which might be, "What pressures did Braithwaite undergo at Greenslade School?" Moreover, even if the pupils do learn the lesson's purpose, will they retain it for an examination—and, further, is that the criterion by which we judge whether learning has occurred? The exam is surely a measuring device but not an especially scientific one. I have found that on occasion pupils who appreciate and understand a piece of literature do not fare well on an exam, whereas some who, in my judgment, do not understand the literature occasionally do score well on the exam. The point is that although there are acceptable ways for teachers to show that they have achieved a lesson's aim, there is really no sure method of measuring the accomplishment. That being the case and this being a manual to explain and exhibit classroom techniques, not examine the philosophical foundation for education, we need to move on to examine ways teachers might achieve their aim at the end of a lesson. Such an accomplishment should incorporate the following components of acceptable conclusion technique:

1. Summarize reasons and examples given during the lesson.
2. Restate the lesson's aim and the answer.

The behavioral objective—that "instrument" by which the teacher "measures" learning—takes this procedure a step further. As the period nears the final moments, the teacher may ask,

1. "What points have we made this period?" Then,
2. "What enabled us to realize this?" Then,
3. "Therefore, as we examine our aim for this period (written on the board), how may it be answered, especially in light of what we considered in class today?"
4. The teacher may require the class to express itself orally or in writing. The writing, on completion, may be shared with the class or collected by the teacher.

Summary

This section showed techniques of handling the various parts of a standard lesson plan:

1. Aims and objectives
2. Motivation
3. Activities
4. Medial summary
5. Achievement of aim and objective

Homework assignments will be discussed in later pages.

Notes

1. For further information on symposia, the reader may consult the following:
   a. Griffith, F., Nelon, C., & Stasheff, E. (1979). *Your speech* (3rd ed., p. 234). New York: Harcourt, Brace, Jovanovich.
   b. Samovar, L. A., & Mills, J. (1980). *Oral communication: Message and response* (4th ed., pp. 220-222). Dubuque, IA: William C. Brown.
   c. Verderber, R. (1994). *The challenge of effective speaking* (9th ed., pp. 411-412). Belmont, CA: Wadsworth.
2. For further information on panel discussions, the reader may consult
   a. Galvin, C., & Book, C. (1975). *Person to person* (pp. 144-148). Skokie, IL: National Textbook.
   b. Samovar, L. A., & Mills, J. (1980). *Oral communication: Message and response* (4th ed., pp. 222-228). Dubuque, IA: William C. Brown.

5

Studying Vocabulary in Context

When I was a college student, one of my educational psychology professors mentioned that when her son asked her or her husband the meaning of a word, they told him immediately, rather than requiring that he look it up. Her theory was that if the boy was reading and needed to know a definition, it would be best to supply it at the moment he could fit it into context. This made sense to me.

Yet when I became a high school teacher, at the commencement of each new semester I was always given, among other materials, a "vocabulary list" and a separate "spelling list" to study with my students during the semester. Always a good soldier, I taught from these lists, without context, even though the concept didn't make sense to me. For example, I always wondered who decided that *photogenic* was a word for 9th-grade students and *zenith* one for 11th-grade students. Some time later in my career, at a department conference to revise and update those lists, I discovered how arbitrary the selections were. Without logic, teachers merely said, "Let's drop this one," or "Let's add that one." This made no sense to me.

In the early 1980s we developed another idea—a specialized list of vocabulary words, culled by surveyors of SAT exams. This list included only those words that appeared most frequently on those college aptitude tests. The logic behind the effort was increased pupil motivation, so we sallied forth to teach to the exam, always considered an educational and philosophical no-no.

The theory behind vocabulary lists, even the SAT list, never worked for me despite my best efforts, ranging from giving homework assignments in vocabulary to playing classroom games with the words. I believe, from my observations and readings, that learning vocabulary by rote is merely tedious. Pupils forget meanings if they are not applied; unlike memorizing "To be, or not to be . . .," there is no poetic beauty behind reciting 25 unconnected words and their definitions. Even if doing so improves SAT scores (a laudable goal), which it might, the words are likely to be forgotten shortly after the exam or never used properly in context!

My personal conclusion, although I must confess continued difficulty in getting adolescents to learn vocabulary, is that words are best taught in context. Therefore, I have abandoned teaching from vocabulary lists and I have begun teaching words from the literature being studied. One problem that does develop from dropping vocabulary lists is that pupils may study the same words over several semesters. Creators of vocabulary lists are usually careful to avoid repetition. However, occasional repetition is not a bad educational technique, and my experience to date has shown that only a few words are taught several times because they appear in books taught in different terms.

More serious problems arise, however. For example, how many vocabulary words should be taught in a semester, when should the words be taught, and what happens if we choose literature that does not include words unfamiliar to teenagers? For example, Arthur Miller's plays, containing simple, everyday language, are totally different from Thomas Hardy's novels, which are filled with eloquent, descriptive prose.

What has, in part, worked for me is to be sure to select at least one piece of literature each semester in which the vocabulary is somewhat elevated. The following is a partial list of such books containing elevated vocabulary:

Jane Eyre by Charlotte Brontë
Wuthering Heights by Emily Brontë
The Call of the Wild by Jack London
David Copperfield by Charles Dickens
Great Expectations by Charles Dickens
A Tale of Two Cities by Charles Dickens
Cyrano de Bergerac by Edmond Rostand
1984 by George Orwell
The Bluest Eye by Toni Morrison
I Know Why the Caged Bird Sings by Maya Angelou
Ethan Frome by Edith Wharton
Crime and Punishment by Fyodor Dostoevsky
Dr. Jekyll and Mr. Hyde by Robert Louis Stevenson
The Scarlet Letter by Nathaniel Hawthorne
The Red Badge of Courage by Stephen Crane
The Grapes of Wrath by John Steinbeck
Go Tell It on the Mountain by James Baldwin
To Sir, With Love by Eric Braithwaite
The Autobiography of Malcolm X
Lord of the Flies by William Golding
Tess of the D'Urbervilles by Thomas Hardy
Moby Dick by Herman Melville
The Picture of Dorian Gray by Oscar Wilde
Walden by Henry David Thoreau
Any Shakespearean play

The problem then becomes compounded by two other issues: (a) How many words should be selected to be taught from each literary work? (b) What other literary work should be selected in conjunction with the first that might contain many words most adolescents do not know?

In deciding the number of words to be taught, I consider several criteria. First, how long will the pupils have the books? If a teacher is allowed to have the books for 6 weeks rather than 4, obviously more vocabulary may be taught. Second, how many words are the youngsters capable of learning? My preference is to teach adolescents to their limit without giving them an irresolute sense of failure. We want to encourage teenagers to speak and understand language better and to appreciate its potential aesthetic beauty. For some classes, I have required 60 words to be learned in 6 weeks, for others over 100. Much depends on the literature selection.

I used to make the decision about how many words to teach based on the reading levels of the students. As I write these words, educators are dispensing with old theories about homogeneous grouping by intelligence or ability and are placing all pupils into one class. What remains constant, though, is that all pupils are entitled to learn vocabulary in context and be offered texts that provide ample material for vocabulary growth.

Selection of additional literature is a somewhat less serious matter. Usually, after teaching "high-powered" literature (any from the aforementioned list), I select material with simpler language, such as Laurents's *West Side Story*, Miller's *Death of a Salesman*, or Zindel's *The Effect of Gamma Rays on Man-in-the-Moon Marigolds*. In such plays important ideas exist in language adolescents can comprehend without the ever-present company of a dictionary.

In answer, therefore, to how many words should be taught in a semester, I have found that it is beneficial to teach as many as 100 to 125 words or as few as 60 to 70 words at the beginning of the semester. I choose the semester's beginning vocabulary list so that I might return to the words during discussions later in class and give tests on them again—and, perhaps, again.

The question of when to teach vocabulary during the semester is affected by when the teacher has the books and when the teacher decides to teach vocabulary during an individual lesson. Although some teachers incorporate a few words each day during the lesson on the texts in which these words appear, I do not. Despite the obvious benefits of such a lesson, namely, seeing the words actually work during discussion, only a few words may be practiced and learned. Literature such as Golding's *Lord of the Flies* is likely to have 10, 20, or even more unfamiliar words for each lesson prepared. What does the teacher do with the other words? My feeling is that a good literature lesson, although not avoiding defining words or failing to appreciate their intrinsic value in special situations, should not digress from its aim by directing too much time to vocabulary work. Instead separate lessons on such vocabulary need be prepared as an integral part of the literary study.

Selecting Words to Be Taught

Although it seems difficult to avoid being arbitrary about select-ing words, I try to keep to the principle of practicality; that is, to select words that I believe are unfamiliar to adolescents yet are used by today's novelists, journalists, broadcasters, politicians, and so forth. Antiquated words and words less frequently heard are, in my opinion, avoidable when preparing to teach vocabulary from a book such as Wharton's *Ethan Frome*, in which I underscored approximately 300 words I suspected my pupils would not know. To be reasonable, I needed to decide which words to teach and which to avoid. I'm sure my decisions were not always the best, but on the other hand, many of my decisions were very good.

For example, from Chapter 1 of *Ethan Frome* I chose to teach the word *undulation* because it helps clarify the description Wharton offers. But *peristyle* I avoided not because it isn't meaningful to the description but because it is rarely used. I chose the words *tenuous, untrodden, aligned,* and *vexed* to teach because they are words used by educated communicators. I did not include the words *obstinately, insinuation, menace,* and *insubstantial* in my formal teaching because I believe many adolescents have some understanding of them, and part of the purpose of teaching vocabulary is to add new words to a youngster's language. Although I might avoid focusing on a word such as *deign* because of its infrequent appearance in modern Ameri-can usage, I might require the pupils to know the word *wraithe* because it was germane to a mood Wharton was capturing.

Finally, in a book such as *Ethan Frome,* it becomes incumbent on the instructor to teach the use of elevated language in distinguishing characters and affecting the reader.

Assigning the Words

Vocabulary words need to be studied at the appropriate moment, when the pupil is reading them in context. Therefore, even though it makes homework longer and more tedious, it is logical to assign vocabulary for the same evening pupils read the section of literature that contains those words. For example, again using Wharton's *Ethan Frome,* if Chapter 2 of the novel is assigned, the teacher might ask the pupils to define and note the page of text on which the following words appear and to use each word in an original sentence: *grotesque, obscure, incredulous, irresolute, elude, disdain, indignation, suffuse, tremulous,* and *repugnant.* On the following day the teacher should spot-check to see if this job was properly completed.

Strategies to Teach Vocabulary Lessons

Success in getting pupils to improve their vocabulary has, admittedly, been slow for the pupils I've taught. Tests I've administered bear this out. However, I have taught vocabulary in a number of interesting and lively lessons, ranging from games such as vocabulary bees, *Password,* crossword puzzles, *Jeopardy,* and charades, to more formal lessons in which principles of analogy are considered and exemplified.

In recent years I have successfully applied the principles of collaborative learning to my vocabulary lessons. Dividing the class into four groups, I charge each group with responsibility for the study of about six words (more or less). For each word, the members must give a definition, record the page number and sentence in which it is used in the text, and most important, create their own original sentence using the word. They are advised to use a dictionary (I provide one for each group), the literature text, and the previous night's vocabulary homework for assistance.

Once a group has completed its task, members select a recorder to place their results on the board. When all of the words are on the board, corrections and suggestions may be added by other pupils and by the teacher. Pupils may copy corrected boardwork into their notebooks. If time permits, and I have found that it rarely does in such a lesson, the teacher may ask pupils how the day's vocabulary lesson enhanced the section of the text under discussion.

Assessing Learning

The results on tests have suggested to me that my best vocabulary lessons haven't really been successful, assuming, that is, we consider 65% the passing grade on such exams. Whether the vocabulary test has been a 40-minute examination, a 5-minute quiz, or a 10-minute section of a test measuring knowledge of the literature studied, pupils in my classes have not, in general, learned as many of the words as I would have liked, despite having studied them in class and, I hope, at home.

The problem could be any one or all of the following:

1. The lessons are not successful.
2. Our expectations are too high. Perhaps we should lower vocabulary test passing grades to 50%.
3. We teach too many words.
4. We do not motivate properly; studying vocabulary is tedious.
5. We do not devote enough class time to the study of vocabulary.
6. Pupils do not study because they are not encouraged at home.
7. Testing devices are too difficult to interpret.
8. Pupils do not read enough.

Because this manual is not a scientific treatise but simply a handbook based on this teacher's experiences and observations, I will quickly abandon the search for reasons why my pupils' performance on vocabulary examinations has remained poor and instead offer ways I have tested comprehension of words and their meanings.

When I was a new teacher, I made up traditional games. For example, in a word pool at the top of a page, I offered 10 sentences with a blank space in each. On the basis of sentence context, pupils were to select a word from the pool and place it in a sentence.

WORD POOL: dauntless, depreciation, intuition
1. The fireman's _____ behavior was rewarded with a life saved.
2. Cars are not good investments because of their rapid _____.
3. My _____ told me not to trust the salesman.

I also used matching games in which words are set up in one column and definitions in another. Pupils are directed to match the definition to the word.

WORDS	DEFINITIONS
_____1. disillusion	A. as a result

_____2. diagnosis   B. to take away dreams
_____3. consequently   C. decision based on testing

I also occasionally used multiple choice tests. A typical example of such a question follows.

Directions: Write the letter of the word or phrase that comes closest to defining the word on the left.

1. ominous: a. toxic, b. threatening, c. sluggish, d. ruthless

This type of question might also be used by substituting "the opposite of" for "defining the."
Another method I've seen used is sentence completion, as follows.

1. I find it difficult to understand how you can _____ in the village after the adventurous life you have led.
    a. manage, b. desecrate, c. vegetate, d. succumb, e. frolic

The word analogy, seen so frequently on college aptitude exams, might be useful in some vocabulary testing situations in the classroom, for example:

irascible:imperturbable a. avid:dispassionate, b. partisan: zealous, c. arduous:difficult, d. avaricious:greedy, e. vehement: cogent

For many years I resorted to testing students' facility with new vocabulary by giving them a paragraph containing 10 underlined words with many contextual clues. A word pool appeared on the bottom of the paragraph and the pupil was to match a word, by examining its context, to a word or phrase from the word pool. An example follows.

The belief that people were placed on earth to "graze" in the great Garden is foolish and *ingenuous.*[1] It is an idea that should be *expunged*[2] from all literature and its misinterpretations, for it places human beings in the most *mundane*[3] of positions, wasting time and becoming *jaded*[4] from having received without achieving. Whether shy and *taciturn*[5] or extroverted and *loquacious*,[6] a person must have purposeful work. *Vituperative*[7] reaction, after all, comes not only when a man or woman errs but also when such people are bored and exist without meaning. Give me an *urbane*[8] woman with a pen in hand or a *rustic*[9] man among fallen lumber. Prancing through the posies picking pomegranates is a picture to be *obliterated*.[10]

WORD POOL: dull, naive, abusive in language, weary from overindulgence, sophisticated, not given to talk, utterly destroy, completely erase

For a time I merely told my pupils to go home and memorize definitions and then I would dictate words to them on vocabulary tests that allowed them to "spit back" the meanings.

Presently I have been testing vocabulary in my classes by placing approximately 10 words in a pool and requesting that the students select any five of them and either define or use each in a sentence that suggests knowledge of the word. Thus far, I have been receiving better results on these exams than on all the aforementioned techniques.

6

Preparing the Lessons

Choosing the Literature

While choosing literature for a class to study, a teacher is often given guidelines by the department head. One must assume that some care was taken when it was designated that, for example, Zindel's *Pigman* would be taught to 9th-grade students and Solzhenitsyn's *One Day in the Life of Ivan Denisovitch* to 12th-grade students—or that there were some criteria for having freshman study *Romeo and Juliet*, sophomores *A Midsummer Night's Dream*, and seniors *Macbeth, King Lear, Othello,* or *Hamlet*.

The teacher might also consider whether the semester will be devoted to any special genre, culture, era, or universal theme. For example, it had been the tradition in New York City high schools that 11th grade was reserved for the study of American literature of all types and that 12th grade contain "world" literature, with the first half focusing on the British. A teacher may, in addition, adapt the semester or year to a particular theme, for example, world peace, racial harmony, or human dignity. The teacher may also want to emphasize a particular genre of literature such as the novel, biography, or play, although it has always been my thinking that unless a course is a special elective selected by pupils, a variety of literary experiences should be offered.

On a less idealistic plane, and perhaps a more realistic one, the English teacher in a complex high school might have to select literature based solely on what is available. With five classes to teach, two or three of which are usually on different grade levels, time and availability count. For example, wanting to teach Wright's *Black Boy* to ninth graders, teachers might discover that four other ninth-grade teachers have already requested the book and there are none left. Alternatively, teachers may find only 35 copies of the book, when they have been assigned two or three freshman classes, each needing 35 copies. Therefore, only one class can study *Black Boy* and the other class must study another book. This expands the workload for the teacher, who must now prepare yet another literary work for the remaining ninth graders.

Finally, it often helps if teachers have already read or studied the literature they select to teach. Sometimes, though infrequently during my career, teachers will know over the summer what classes they will teach in the fall. More likely than not, however, only a few days' notice will be given to teachers before they are expected to do extensive preparation.

These practical matters are important to selecting literature to be taught. Although we aspire to choose literature based on the intellectual needs of our pupils, we are too often constrained by limits such as availability and time. There are time limits on how long the teacher may retain the books. If, for example, a teacher feels the need to spend 8 to 10 weeks on *King Lear* but is in possession of 70 texts for only 6 weeks, an obvious problem exists.

I recommend being idealistic and selecting a variety of genres within a semester's special theme, geared to the needs of the pupils. Also helpful is maintaining an ability to mutter privately about how ridiculous it is that we don't have ample preparation time or enough books for everyone. (This suggestion is meant only to relieve temporary frustration. I do not meant to imply that a teacher should not "make noise." Public righteous indignation is the only way to improve conditions. Teachers should squawk!)

Reading the Literature

Saying that the selected literature needs to be read seems superfluous. Yet I submit that reading for understanding, self-knowledge, and personal pleasure is different from reading to teach values, stylistic technique, appreciation, vocabulary, and so forth, to adolescents. What I do to prepare to teach a book is to read it once for pleasure and impressions. Next I do a second reading, during which time I underline vocabulary words that I believe will be unfamiliar to my prospective pupils and I bracket passages that I believe will be fruitful to read aloud or to assign during classroom activities. Both during and after this perusal, I record in a notebook ideas, themes, concepts, techniques, values, and questions that the book seems to advance. I then examine what I've recorded and eliminate whatever seems extraneous or irrelevant, while focusing on what I will retain and, ultimately, present during my lessons. I am not reluctant to consult with colleagues who have taught the book in the past. When there is enough time, I visit the library for additional source material that might even be used for supplementary assignments.

Spacing the Lessons

The question of how many lessons should be taught on a piece of literature must be answered. I have taught *Romeo and Juliet* in 15 lessons, and *Lord of the Flies* in 11; *Hamlet* generally takes me approximately 25 lessons, whereas *Ethan Frome* has taken me but 10. I have taught Hemingway's *The Old Man and the Sea* in 3 lessons, but I have a colleague who teaches it in 10. I have taught *To Kill a Mockingbird* in 6 lessons, but I have also taught it in 16. I have taken nearly as long to teach *Death of a Salesman* as to teach *Moby Dick*. Much depends on my personal interpretations of the work and what I believe my pupils need to know and consider.

Once I determine approximately how many lessons I will teach on a specific book, I need to figure out how to assign pages for pupils to read. Authors do not write with high school lessons in mind; thus the task becomes somewhat sticky. If I want to teach my pupils about Richard Wright's ability to capture the essence of the streets of Chicago and a poor, black, teenage boy, how many pages must they read before the lesson to be knowledgeable during the lesson's presentation? The pages assigned must include the information pertinent to the lesson's aim and activities. How many pages may be assigned? If students are given one night to complete homework, 30 to 40 pages does not seem unreasonable, but if a longer assignment is given, pupils should be offered more time to finish. I feel no remorse in assigning more than 100 pages, if necessary, for a weekend. The exact number of pages assigned is arbitrary, of course, based on what I've seen my esteemed colleagues of the past assign and the length of time I will have the books. The number of pages to assign is clearly not set in stone. I do believe that students tend to rise to the level of expectations. If I require less, I will surely get less!

Lengthier assignments that require allowing students additional days to read before a specific lesson is taught create the problem of teaching other material between lessons on the literature under study. During those days I usually teach lessons on vocabulary from the text. Alternatively, I may teach a writing skills lesson from which a composition may result. I also assign supplementary literature, and I might choose to discuss such matter on days that my pupils are completing work prior to their next in-class literature lesson.

The Lessons

The first literature lesson of a series includes the distribution of books. The purpose of the lesson is to engender excitement and to provide a reason to read my first assignment, which always accompanies this premiere presentation. This persuasive lesson, as every lesson to follow, should ideally contain aim or objective, motivation, activity, medial summary, activity, final summary and conclusion, and a homework assignment (examples appear in the Resources). Such an introduction, meant to encourage reading, should involve most if not all of the following important elements:

1. Immediate arousal of interest
2. Mention of some exposition
3. Mention of main characters
4. Mention of setting and time
5. Suggestion of major complication

6. Mention of possible obstacles to reading
7. Arousal of suspense

After completing preparation for the motivating lesson, the teacher should consider what to teach in the next lesson, which will begin on the first page of the literature and cover anywhere between 10 and 60 pages. "What exists in these pages that needs to be taught to my pupils?" is the question I ask myself. For example, if I were about to teach the first couple of scenes of *The Glass Menagerie,* I might answer that question with, "I want my pupils to get a feeling for the time and setting," thereby beginning to establish my aim and even my objective for this next lesson. I follow that procedure for each successive lesson.

Once my aim and objective for a lesson are created, I plan the day's activities. These activities must assist me in achieving the lesson's aim, while enabling my pupils to think and do. I keep in mind that activities must be varied to avoid boredom. As previously mentioned, "Take out your books and read from page _____ to _____" repeated daily is tedium we can do without. Lessons should be varied. Some may be of the traditional pivotal question-answer type, interspersed with others based on collaborative learning. Some lessons should require reading and scrutiny; others should incorporate pupil planning and performance.

All lessons, however, must require homework: a reading assignment with ample time for completion, questions that require thinking and writing to answer, and vocabulary (if necessary) to define. Vocabulary, as previously mentioned, may be discussed during a literature lesson, and I believe it is appropriate to focus on unclear words, especially when pupils want to know them, even during a lesson for which the aim is other than vocabulary expansion. But as also previously mentioned, I believe focus on vocabulary should be left to selected lessons so proper attention can be devoted to accomplishing the aims of the particular lesson at hand.

Homework, however, involves a different philosophical base. Homework is an exercise given to challenge students to think and to offer them practice in both reading and writing skills. Furthermore, it is a challenge to their sense of responsibility. Too many pupils do their homework hastily, poorly, or not at all. Therefore, it becomes important that teachers do their best to encourage students to complete homework thoroughly and with pride. The suggestions that follow, some ideal, some not, are tactics I and many of my colleagues have used to help convince adolescents to do homework.

1. Build the lesson in such a way that the homework reveals answers for questions the teacher has suspensefully posed. A simple example: "Considering what we read in Act I of *Death of a Salesman*, what does the final scene of the act suggest about what will happen in Act II? Will the Lomans' lives improve? Explain."

2. Make answers to homework a vital part of the next day's lesson. The teacher may provide as a routine activity an opportunity for pupils to read homework answers aloud during or after the motivation. The answers should logically move the lesson toward achieving its objective. Praise and encouragement for pupil responses must be generously provided.

3. Check homework routinely by collecting entire class sets, collecting several homework assignments arbitrarily from each class, or some other method. My pupils have rarely been motivated, despite my "brilliant" efforts, to do homework regularly unless they are rewarded in some way.

4. I have found it somewhat necessary to punish failure to complete homework. Despite psychologists' insistence that praise be the cause of improvement, my experience has led me to believe that letting people get away with shirking responsibility teaches them that this negative behavior is an acceptable way of life. Although I am not opposed to giving pupils ample time to make up missed work—when a pupil offers a good excuse—I always establish strict guidelines and make a sincere effort to stand by them regarding the number of missed homework assignments allowed before grade reduction or failure result and how much time is allowed to make up homework (usually no more than a day).

5. Administer surprise quizzes (sometimes on a daily basis). Such tests reveal whether pupils have read the previous night's assignment. A question such as, "Where does Travis sleep?" is more appropriate on such a quiz than "What do you believe

is troubling the Younger family in the first scene of *A Raisin in the Sun?*"

6. Use phone calls and letters to parents when pupils do not do homework.
7. Make the assignment reasonable and "doable." The assignment should not require pupils to discover solutions they cannot conceive. Homework should not require an amount of time that detracts an adolescent from other class assignments, home chores, or leisure activities. Generally homework should not take less than a half hour or longer than an hour to complete.
8. Teachers should exhibit exemplary behavior regarding preparation. Lessons should be researched, homework and other assignments checked and returned on a timely basis. I require nothing of my students that I do not require of myself—and I am not above my own rules established for their benefit.

Numerous examples of various homework assignments can be found in the Resources.

Use of VCRs

Bringing literature to life is a wonderful experience. The VCR is a blessing! I have witnessed pupils, after studying a literary work in my class, transfixed by the screen production. A case in point occurred several years ago when one of our school's star basketball players, hardly known for being a scholar, was the last one to leave my class—even though the bell had rung—because he insisted on seeing the Danes carry Hamlet's dead body to the top of the tower. The young man had forgotten he had a basketball strategy meeting and practice, and when, several moments later, his coach came worriedly to my room asking for him, I merely pointed to the rear of the room. "I can't believe this. What did you do to him?" was the coach's astounded utterance.

What I had done was to challenge him and his peers to about 8 weeks of readings, questions, homework, analogies, vocabulary, and so on—and then offer them a performance of what may be the greatest play ever written. Although not all my pupils reach the same level of intense enjoyment as that particular athlete, I have observed that the majority of my pupils, *after* studying a literary work, benefit greatly from the performance.

I never show the performance before the study of the work is completed because it reveals too much material I use to create suspense to motivate reading. Moreover, a difficult work, such as a Shakespearean play, or a Brontë or Hardy novel, first needs a discussion of historical background, exposition, mood, vocabulary, and so forth.

Once the literature has been scrutinized, though, pupils are ready to see it on their own terms. The VCR must be procured several weeks in advance, usually for four 40-minute periods for movies from 2 to 2½ hours long. I always tell my students that the movie is being shown to them mainly for their enjoyment, because that is a great part of why we read and study literature—not only for self-edification. Although I do not want to apply pressure to their enjoyment, I do advise them that their examination will require knowledge of the film. I insist on total silence during the showing and nearly all the students comply.

Assessments

Testing a pupil's knowledge of a literary experience serves a number of purposes, the least of which is to gain a criterion for an "objective" evaluation of the pupil. Unfortunately, the very nature of the examination process is tension producing, but I believe it is a teacher's duty to reduce that pressure to a minimum, even though it is impossible to eliminate it entirely.

I envision and despise the thought of a pupil memorizing lists of facts or concepts and their supports, only to forget them 5 minutes after submitting the completed exam to the proctor. The high school literature examination should be another opportunity for pupils to apply logic to carefully devised questions. The exam affords students another situation in which to think, review, and consider what they've learned from the long study process they've undergone. The testing experience should not be pressure filled; it should be challenging, positive, and perhaps in some way enjoyable. Of course, yes, the teacher should be able to partially measure, from pupil responses, which lessons need to be changed (as all lessons are eventually

altered through updating and new insights) and how much knowledge pupils have gained from having studied the literature.

Tests should not be geared to cause failure. Large measures of
success should be possible during the testing experience. On the
other hand, it mustn't be something to be taken lightly. The test must
require discussion, review at home, individual study, and study
among peers. Encouraging thought and conversation about the literature is, after all, a prime objective of a literature exam. The objective
of the exam is not to fail pupils or, in my opinion, to achieve a bell
curve. The objective is to provide an outlet for adolescents to show
their knowledge, to think logically, to have fun, and to succeed.

How often should pupils be "entitled" to such "fun?" Several
criteria need to be considered to answer this question:

1. Will one major test, at the completion of the literary study,
   enable the students to express enough about the work?
2. Will one major test place too much pressure on pupils?
3. Will too many tests place too much pressure on pupils?
4. Will too many tests cause pupils to forget what they studied
   immediately after each exam?
5. Has enough of the literature been taught for the exam to serve
   as both review and reinforcement?

I have used, during my career, enough methods to learn that I
cannot satisfy all the pupils' needs. I do not give one major examination exclusively. Rather, after a portion of the literature has been
taught, students are required to record their thoughts about it for
evaluation. Usually, for a play, I give a test after the conclusion of each
act. For a novel or biography, I prepare anywhere from two to four
exams, spaced strategically and judiciously apart to permit study
time, review, and absorption of ideas. Specifically, if a book takes 20
lessons to complete, an exam every 6 or 7 lessons might suffice.

I believe wholeheartedly that literature exams should only be of
the essay type. Matching games, fill-ins, multiple choice, and other
types of short answers are not good teaching devices. They force
pupils to commit names, events, and so forth to memory for a brief
period of time, only to be forgotten shortly thereafter. Sometimes,
such exams are too easy; more often, I have personally found them

nitpickingly difficult. Again, the point of the examination is not to be a temporary exercise but a learning experience during which pupils may not only exhibit but also apply their knowledge.

I do give short-answer tests combined with questions requiring brief essays to pupils whose poor writing skills would cause them considerable failure on total essay tests. However, most of my tests remain strictly essay, which presents the problem of an overloaded marking schedule at home. Essays must be evaluated not merely for content but for organization, grammar, and structure, also which takes additional time.

My favorite format for a literature examination is one that involves 4 days of preparation and collaborative learning on the part of the pupils. I apply this type of exam only at the completion of an entire work of literature. On the first of these 4 days, the pupils are divided into four groups with between six and eight people in each group. Each group is then charged with creating two questions about the literature that need answers requiring thought, explanation, and textual support. When a group completes its questions, it seeks approval from the teacher. The teacher peruses each question and checks to see that it does not repeat the whole or part of another group's questions. The teacher should also consider whether a question can be responded to in a thoughtful essay rather than in a mere few sentences. The question, "How does Hamlet escape Claudius's death sentence?" requires, on the surface, only several sentences of factual explanation. On the other hand, the question, "How does Hamlet's intelligence delay him from obtaining his revenge?" is a question that demands contemplation and scrutiny of the text, class discussion, and notes. Once eight questions are developed and accepted (usually a 20- to 25-minute process), the groups exchange them and attempt to answer them. Homework for the day is to answer each of the two questions provided by the other groups.

On the second day, the students reassemble in their groups. They are allocated 10 to 15 minutes to share their homework and to prepare a report in response to their peers' questions that will be delivered to the rest of the class. One or two pupils from each group read these responses to the class, which is required to take notes. This part of the lesson, which runs through the rest of the period, frequently includes pupils demanding that the readers speak slower and repeat ideas. Often, they ask questions and pupils from other groups, the speaker, or I will answer. Because the "givens" in this type of test condition allow the pupils to have their books open, pupils frequently request that speakers mention the page numbers in the text from which they developed support for their answers. Before the conclusion of the period, pupils seem almost frantically involved in discussing the many issues that arose during the study of the literature. This lesson serves as pupil review for the examination that will take place on the following day, the third of this 4-day testing experience.

On test days, pupils are required to write three essays selected from the eight questions posed. Although I insist they study all eight of the issues raised and advise them that the three essays they will be required to write will be selected by the teacher, I usually mitigate the task and allow the pupils, on the day of the exam, to choose to answer the three questions with which they are most comfortable. In this way pupils may fill a 40-minute period with private thoughts (there's not a spare moment for them to cheat) about a major work of literature.

The final day of this 4-day procedure comes only after the teacher has evaluated all the essays. In general, I will assign an essay containing no textual references and no quoted material no grade higher than a C, despite accuracy of content. Moreover, if a pupil totally disregards style and structure (I do remain very liberal in my judgment of this because of the time constraint under which they labor), I deduct an additional 10 points from their total score. Each essay receives a separate grade, with comments on both content and style. Letter grades are given numerical equivalents (e.g., C = 75%), then added and divided by 3 and transcribed back into a letter grade (e.g., 79% = C+).

The lesson has several aims on the day graded exams are distributed to the pupils. The first is to review the literature a final time. The second is to encourage the pupils to do well. The third is to encourage the improvement of good writing. First, I find praiseworthy items to mention about the test results as a whole, perhaps calling on several pupils to read all or portions of their essays that are exemplary. Then I make two or three suggestions on how the exams could have been better. Next I distribute a brief exercise that contains errors in writing culled from the examination papers. Pupils are expected to work on the examples individually. Once completed, we briefly go over the exercise. I then distribute the exam and circulate among the pupils, assisting those who ask for my help. I will discuss only issues, whether the questions are content or style oriented. I do not discuss the grade. Usually I do not give homework on the day before we embark on our next literary journey. To require more questions on the book just tested seems to me to be overkill. Moreover, by now I feel I have, indeed, given my pupils a thorough and good experience!

Resources

Loving Literature

The Plan in Action

1. While examining the Resources, the reader should keep in mind pages 66-68 of the text regarding homework. The teacher may check or collect homework in a number of ways. In these lessons note the frequency with which the pupils must rely on the previous night's homework to achieve a successful lesson for the day.

2. Throughout the Resources the reader may note that answers have been supplied for certain questions. When the answer was not supplied it was because it was, in my opinion, either literal or easily interpreted.

3. During the presentation of any lessons herein, the teacher may feel at liberty to collect pupil writing or homework. However, I strongly believe that such collection obligates the teacher of English to evaluate both content and style of the work, not merely to place a check on it!

Resource A

Lesson Plans for
Markandaya's *Nectar in a Sieve*

Prepared for a 10th-grade class

In 1988 I taught Kamala Markandaya's (1954) *Nectar in a Sieve* to a 10th-grade class. The book was sandwiched between two other novels. The first piece of literature I taught to them that semester was Paton's *Cry, the Beloved Country* and I completed the semester with Buck's *The Good Earth*. I was not only able to teach philosophical concepts, but I shared a role with a social studies colleague by requiring assignments that incorporated knowledge of the countries in the literature under scrutiny. In fact, I collaborated with the social studies teacher who shared most of my pupils so that our work would not be duplicated and pupils would derive maximum benefit from our efforts.

The concept of interdisciplinary teaching is no longer new, and it has proven beneficial in helping young people begin to see more sense to their world, which all too often seems illogical and chaotic. The logistics of establishing such a program, however, usually lie in the hands of the school's programmer. This process is subject matter for another text. Here, though, it is necessary to say that a high school literature teacher working in conjunction with a high school social studies teacher can help pupils recognize the literature in historical perspective, gain insights into the tenor of the time and place in which authors lived, and understand the natures of particular cultures as they formed, grew, survived, or perished. Interdisciplinary teaching can encourage pupils to perceive better what is occurring around their own lives, render predictions about what they anticipate for their future, and make suggestions about what they might do to improve their situation both in the present and future.

The collaboration I and my social studies colleague shared was based on our mutual agreement rather than a school-approved and school-advertised program. Initially we made the decision based on the fact that we shared many of the same pupils and, coincidentally, all those who were in one of my classes were also in only one of his classes.

The lessons to follow were made during a time when many educators began touting collaborative learning as the wave of all future teaching. Therefore, amidst an inundation of peripheral work, including viewing Richard Attenborough's 1982 film, *Gandhi,* writing a composition based on Indian philosophy, and researching an aspect of Indian culture in preparation for a 3-minute oral presentation, *Nectar in a Sieve* took 10 lessons of the collaborative learning style to complete. In addition to the composition and supplementary cultural report, vocabulary work was also assigned and collected. One examination on the text was given on completion of the literary study.

The text used for these lessons was Markandaya, K. (1954). *Nectar in a sieve.* New York: Harper & Row. All page numbers refer to this edition.

Supplementary Assignment

On (date), (usually 4 weeks from the day the assignment is given) you will be expected to speak extemporaneously[1] on an aspect of India. Research and practice are mandatory to achieving excellence. Although no written document will be collected, you must mention, during the speech, at least three sources from which you gathered your information. You may make comparisons of India to South Africa (about which we just read) and to our own USA. Follow news reports, if possible, that discuss what is happening in India today. Time limit for speech: 3 minutes.

On 6 successive days Attenborough's (1982) film *Gandhi* is shown. On the first day of the showing, the following assignment appears on the board or is distributed to each pupil. This sheet is distributed during the lesson motivating the students to read the book.

You are being asked to do more than merely watch and enjoy *Gandhi*. You are expected to intelligently observe life in India as it existed during Gandhi's era. Each night at home you are to date a page and write approximately 100 words on what you observed in the day's segment of *Gandhi*. Avoid completely any comments about acting, directing, filming, and so forth. Discuss only what you observed about India. Allusions to scenes from the film to support your statements are important. At the conclusion of the film you should have a six-page journal that will be collected and evaluated. Because we will be studying a novel set in India that was written by a woman native to the country and no video of the book exists, *Gandhi* will serve to supply the flavor necessary to understand and empathize better with the feelings stressed in the novel.

Note

1. *Extemporaneous* implies that you may use notes when you speak. Charts, diagrams, maps, graphs, and statistics are welcome. Reading a speech word-for-word will assuredly result in reduced interest from your audience and great disappointment from your teacher.

Aim: How can we narrow the focus of our supplementary research?

Objective: Pupils will work in groups to form questions about aspects of Indian culture.

1. We will soon be studying a novel set in India. To gain a more complete appreciation of the book, each of you will be required to report on an aspect of Indian culture in an extemporaneous speech of approximately 3 minutes on (date). Libraries are well stocked with materials on this subject. Do not confine yourself to one source. Use a minimum of three.
2. Teacher writes on board:

Aspects of a Nation's Culture

   a. Historical development
   b. Politics
   c. Religion
   d. Goods and services
   e. Education
   f. Economics
   g. Climate and geography

3. Teacher forms the class into four groups at random. Each group is to select a topic and then devise subtopics for each member to avoid duplication. A member of each group must give the teacher a list of the group's members and the subjects on which each will be speaking.
4. Teacher distributes assignment.
5. Teacher assists each group as necessary and collects lists at end of period.

Homework

Begin researching as soon as possible.

Aim: How can we prepare to write an essay on the topic, the philosophy of acceptance in a world of suffering?

Objective: Pupils will begin preparing an outline on this subject.

1. Teacher writes three quotations on board:
   a. "We are taught to bear our sorrows in silence, and all this is so that the soul may be cleansed" (Markandaya, 1954, p. 116).
   b. "Oh, earth, you're too beautiful for anybody to realize you" (Wilder in Nagelberg, 1948, p. 149).
   c. Whatever happens is for the best (Hillel).
   Students interpret meanings of these statements.
2. The Greeks coined a term for the idea that seems to be generating from these lines. Teacher places on board *stoicism:* belief that what happens on earth was meant to be and cannot and should not be changed.
3. Medial summary: Although many people are stoic in outlook, how do you feel about a beautiful man like Stephan Kumalo, from *Cry, the Beloved Country,* forced to feel less human than others? Or how do you feel about South African blacks, in general, who have been separated from and by whites, or about Jews, many of whom were exterminated—or about any group subjugated or enslaved?
4. Teacher reads following line from *Nectar in a Sieve.* "Acquiescent imbeciles, do you think spiritual grace comes from being in want, or from suffering? What thoughts have you when your belly is empty or your body is sick? Tell me that they are noble and I will call you a liar. Go before I am too entangled in your philosophies" (p. 116). These words are in response to the first quotation on the board taken from *Nectar in a Sieve.* React to this idea.
5. Write a 50-word paragraph suggesting which philosophy you lean toward—action or acceptance.
6. Pupils share ideas.
7. Begin outlining your ideas for tomorrow's essay. Rely on readings, personal experiences, historical knowledge, and observations for the body of the work.

Homework

Prepare to complete a 250-word essay in class tomorrow on the philosophy of acceptance in a world of suffering. (The next day pupils write the essay. Several days later, no more than 4, the essays are returned and are the focus of a writing improvement lesson.)

Aim: Why is Kamala Markandaya's *Nectar in a Sieve* an important novel to study?

Objective: Pupils will read the first several pages of *Nectar in a Sieve.*

1. Teacher places the following quotation on the board.

> . . . now our young people must take another step and assume responsibility for their parents, their college teachers, their younger brothers and sisters, and on outward into society, to all those who seem to be enemies but are only the deceived, the broken and the lost.
>
> *Reich, 1971, p. 321*

   Students discuss their interpretations of the line.

2. What is a person supposed to do? Should Americans, for example, give up a sizable portion of their earnings, go to work in a loincloth, and eat only enough to survive so that no one in the world will be hungry?

3. What should you do? What is reasonable for us to do for the deprived, not only in a country like India but right here in America?

4. Americans, especially New Yorkers, take much for granted. We tend to believe that what we do, everyone should do—the way we work, marry, raise children, eat, and measure time. What is your reaction to this?

5. *Nectar in a Sieve* is a book about India, a culture vastly different from ours. Teacher distributes texts and book receipts.

6. What is the meaning of the title? See page 5 (Coleridge quotation from which the title is derived).

7. Knowing that the story deals with Indians and having seen *Gandhi,* written an essay on an Indian philosophy, and begun research on an aspect of Indian culture, what do you anticipate the book will involve? Teacher writes on board:

Themes From Nectar in a Sieve

   a. Hard work and blind faith
   b. Family loyalty and love
   c. Stoic acceptance
   d. Industrialization
   e. Male supremacy/delineated roles
   f. Hunger and poverty
   g. Man vs. nature

h. Prejudice and greed
i. Survival
j. Debasement
k. Pride and dignity

(Teacher should make every effort to phrase boardwork in pupil-composed language.)

8. You will meet many characters with Indian names and some with American names. Teacher writes on board:

Characters From Nectar in a Sieve

a. Rukmani: narrator and mother
b. Nathan: her husband
c. Ira: their daughter
d. Arjun, Thambi, Murgan, Sunja: their sons
e. Kenny: white doctor and humanitarian
f. Old Granny
g. Biswa: money lender
h. Kunthi, Kali: neighbors' wives
i. Sacrakani: albino child of Ira

9. Teacher distributes vocabulary assignment.
10. Begin reading Chapter 1. What do the first two pages imply about the author other than that she is old?

Homework

1. Read pages 7 through 28 of *Nectar in a Sieve.*
2. Answer the following:
   a. Describe the customs under which Rukmani was married. What is your opinion of them? (Chapter 1)
   b. Clearly the author loves and respects her husband. Describe the type of behavior he displays that most Americans would likely despise. (Chapter 2)
   c. What hints are in Chapter 3 to suggest times will grow worse for the protagonists?

Vocabulary Assignment

(To be distributed to each pupil)

In reading *Nectar in a Sieve* to prepare for class discussions, I underlined 318 words that I suspected you may not know. To study all these words would be a prodigious, in fact, an unrealistic task that would distract us from the vital issues in the book. Therefore on (<u>date</u>) please submit a list of 100 vocabulary words with which you are unfamiliar from Markandaya's *Nectar in a Sieve*. The finished product must take the following form:

1. Word
2. Page of appearance in text
3. Definition
4. Creative sentence demonstrating understanding of word

This work will be collected and evaluated for accuracy, thoroughness, and neatness.

Routine Daily Lessons for Study of *Nectar in a Sieve*

Aims will vary from one day to the next, but objectives will remain constant.

1. Students will be assigned to groups. Each group will be presented a line or lines taken verbatim from the text. Each group must select a recorder and a spokesperson, who must change every day. The spokesperson will present to the class, near the completion of the lesson,
   a. The group's interpretation of the line or lines from the text
   b. Circumstances surrounding the line or lines
   c. Group and individual opinions of circumstances, intentions, and implications of the line or lines
   (The sheet of instructions that follows is distributed to each student.)
2. The rest of the class may take notes on the presentation or may challenge interpretations through questions or textual references.
3. Time allotment
   a. Group meetings: 10 to 15 minutes
   b. Presentations: 5 minutes per group
4. Summary and achievement of aim will occur at the period's end, when the teacher points to the aim written on the board and says, "Please respond to our day's aim in writing. Base your paragraph on today's group presentations."
5. Homework assignments appear on the printed instructions distributed daily. Each day the teacher will collect homework from one group and do an in-class check of homework on another group.

Instructions to Pupils Regarding
Collaboration Approach to *Nectar in a Sieve*

Each day your group will be asked to consider quoted material from Markandaya's book. You will have no more than 15 minutes to prepare a presentation that will be delivered to the class. Each day you are to select a different person to record group ideas and a different person to present them. Within the presentation the spokesperson must discuss the following:

> a. The group's interpretation of the quotation based on its meaning in the text
> b. Circumstances surrounding the quoted material
> c. Personal impressions (group and individual) of the quoted material's meaning

The entire group may be called on to answer questions from the class. The spokesperson for the day should be sure to speak clearly so the class may note important features of the presentation. Approximately 5 minutes will be allocated for each group presentation.

(For discussion of problems associated with collaborative learning approach to teaching literature, please refer to page 45 of the text.)

Aim: How do marriage customs, childbearing, and child raising differ in Rukmani's India from our New York City?

Objective: Pupils will work in groups to prepare and deliver oral presentations from which peers may take notes and ask questions.

Group 1: page 12

You are not a child anymore.

Group 2: page 15

Well, so long as you don't forget you are pregnant.

Group 3: page 17

That was typical of my husband: when he had worked things out for himself he would follow his conclusions at whatever cost to himself. I am sure it could not have been easy for him to see his wife more learned than he himself was, for Nathan could not even write his name; yet not once did he assert his rights and forbid me my pleasure, as lesser men might have done.

Group 4: page 26

In our sort of family it is well to be the first born: what resources there are have later to be shared out in smaller and smaller portions.

Homework

1. Read pages 29 through 49 of *Nectar in a Sieve.*
2. Answer the following:
   a. What immediate effects does the tannery have on the village? (Chapter 4)
   b. Why is Rukmani nervous with Kenny in her home? (Chapter 5)
   c. Describe and give your opinion of Ira's wedding day. (Chapter 6)
   d. In what ways does the monsoon reduce the family's sense of morality? (Chapter 7)

Aim: By what philosophies do the characters live that you might like to see in America?

Objective: Pupils will work in groups to prepare and deliver oral presentations from which peers may take notes and ask questions.

Group 1: page 32

Foolish woman, there is no going back. Bend, like the grass, that you do not break.

Group 2: page 36

Yet I thought you would know better, who live by the land yet think of taking from it without giving.

Group 3: page 47

Never mind what you thought! Is this not a time of scarcity? Can you buy rice anywhere else? Am I not entitled to charge more for that? Two ollocks will I let you have and that is charity.

Group 4: pages 47 and 48

Meanwhile you will suffer and die, you meek, suffering fools. Why do you keep this ghastly silence?

Homework

1. Read pages 50 through 66 of *Nectar in a Sieve*.
2. Answer the following:
   a. What is your opinion of Kunthi's plans to supplement her income? (Chapter 8)
   b. What is your opinion of Ira's husband for returning her? (Chapter 9)
   c. What is your opinion of the family for celebrating? (Chapter 10)
   d. What possible jealousy could arise in Chapter 11? Why? Why doesn't it occur?

Aim: What differences exist in relationships between men and women in Rukmani's India and present-day New York City?

Objective: Pupils will work in groups to prepare and deliver oral presentations from which peers may take note and ask questions.

Group 1: page 51

Let her be! She is a trollop, and is anxious only that there should be a supply of men.

Group 2: page 54

I do not blame him. He is justified, for a man needs children. He has been patient.

Group 3: page 56

Indeed they have, over men, and events, and especially over women.

Group 4: page 64

Your husband would give much to know where you have been tonight.

Homework

1. Read pages 67 through 96 of *Nectar in a Sieve.*
2. Answer the following:
   a. Why are Arjun and Thambi fired? What do they decide? How will this affect the family? (Chapter 12)
   b. Describe how the drought affects the family. (Chapter 13)
   c. What is your opinion of Nathan after learning of his secret? (Chapter 14)
   d. What eludes the family when the people come to settle Saja's death? (Chapter 15)

Aim: Why does it seem that these characters, who are poor and ignorant, have no spirit or joy in life?

Objective: Pupils will work in groups to prepare and deliver oral presentations from which peers may take notes and ask questions.

Group 1: page 69

What was it we had to learn? To fight against tremendous odds? What was the use? One only lost the little one had. Of what use to fight when the conclusion is known?

Group 2: page 74

I work among you when my spirit wills it. . . . I go when I am tired of your follies and stupidities, your eternal, shameful poverty. I can only take you people in small doses.

Group 3: page 90

I am the father of her sons. She would have told you, and I was weak.

Group 4: page 96

Of course, as my friend has said, it is your loss. But not, remember, our responsibility. Perhaps you may even be better off. . . . You have many mouths to feed, and —

Homework

1. Read pages 97 through 116 of *Nectar in a Sieve.*
2. Answer the following:
    a. What "miracle" does Rukmani discover has been curing Kuti? What is your opinion of Ira? What happens to Kuti? (Chapter 16)
    b. What is your opinion of the family after reading Chapter 17?
    c. What has Jenny apparently decided in Chapter 18?
    d. What good fortune comes to Selvam? (Chapter 19)

Aim: What problems do Nathan and Rukmani encounter with their children?

Objective: Pupils will work in groups to prepare and deliver oral presentations from which peers may take notes and ask questions.

Group 1: page 104

I was grateful enough for the food, but of what she bought Nathan would not touch a morsel.

Group 2: pages 111 and 112

My country. Sometimes I do not know which is my country.

Group 3: page 112

You will feel better when it is born. A baby is no worse for being conceived in an encounter.

Group 4: page 114

Not displeased. Perhaps disappointed, since all our sons have forsaken the land. But it is the best way for you.

Homework

1. Read pages 117 through 139 of *Nectar in a Sieve.*
2. Answer the following:
   a. Why does Rukmani think a child born in wedlock is better than one born out of wedlock? (Chapter 20)
   b. What is Ira's child? How does the family react? What symbolism does such a child suggest? (Chapter 20)
   c. What happens to Old Granny? (Chapter 21)
   d. What pity are we moved to feel in Chapter 22?
   e. What final blow is struck at the family at the end of Part One? What is Selvam's attitude? (Chapter 23)

Aim: What social problems do we see in Rukmani's India that we also see in modern New York City?

Objective: Pupils will work in groups to prepare and deliver oral presentations from which their peers may take notes and ask questions.

Group 1: page 123

Just a matter of coloring, or lack of it. It is only a question of getting used to. Who is to say this color is right and that is not?

Group 2: page 126

Why go on about it? You are only distressing yourself and it might never have been. I tell you a hospital is only for the sick. There is nowhere for the old.

Group 3: page 129

Mother, what is a bastard? Did you wish me to be born? . . . Have I got a father?

Group 4: page 139

It is perpetual shame to me that I have nothing to offer my parents.

Homework

1. Read pages 141 through 166 of *Nectar in a Sieve.*
2. Answer the following:
   a. What is the attitude of the family as they ride to their son? (Chapter 24)
   b. What further loss do they suffer in Chapter 25? Who helps them find their son's home?
   c. What do they learn from their daughter-in-law in Chapter 26? How do they accept the information? What will they do next?

Aim: What evidence of pride do we see in the characters?

Objective: Pupils will work in groups to prepare and deliver oral presentations from which their peers may take notes and ask questions.

Group 1: page 151

Now I shall be wholly indebted to my daughter-in-law.

Group 2: page 155

We may yet be forced to do that, if we do not find our son.

Group 3: pages 163 and 164

Of course you realize he has nothing to do with you. . . . I mean he is not your grandson. . . . One must live.

Group 4: page 166

Servants or not, it is all one! You must use the back gate. Come on, if you are seen here I will lose my job.

Homework

1. Complete *Nectar in a Sieve*.
2. Answer the following:
    a. How does Rukmani earn money for food? What is their plan? How long are they at the temple? Who helps them? Why? (Chapter 27)
    b. Are they earning more money? How? What "extravagances" does Rukmani indulge in? What happens to Nathan? (Chapter 28)
    c. In what way does Nathan tell his wife he will still be with her? Quote the line. (Chapter 29)
    d. What page follows page 189? Explain.
    e. Discuss in 50 to 75 words: Is the novel more depressing than uplifting?

Aim: In what ways are the main characters in this novel exemplary of human strength and dignity?

Objective: Pupils will work in groups to prepare oral presentations to which their peers may take notes and ask questions.

Group 1: page 177

And what would I do there in these green fields of yours I know nothing about! What is more, they are not even yours, do you want me to starve with you?

Group 2: page 187

You are not alone. I live in my children.

Group 3: page 188

I picked up the fragments of my life and put them together, all but the missing piece; and out of my affliction I called to Puli.

Group 4: page 189

Do not worry. We shall manage.

Homework

1. Prepare a test for someone who has just read *Nectar in a Sieve.* The questions should deal with characters, events, and issues. They may be of the short-answer or essay type—or whatever else you can create.
2. Complete your vocabulary study for collection.

Aim: What is important about our study of *Nectar in a Sieve?*

Objective: Pupils will ask and answer their own questions about *Nectar in a Sieve.*

1. This lesson should be almost entirely run by pupils. Groups may meet to select two or three of their best questions from their previous night's homework. They will then pose the questions for the rest of the class to answer.
2. Pupils respond to questions.
3. The teacher may place pertinent information on the board.
4. Class will ask and answer as many questions as possible, which will serve as their review for the upcoming examination on *Nectar in a Sieve.*

Homework

1. Study! Bring both your text and notebook to class. You will be allowed to use both during tomorrow's essay exam on *Nectar in a Sieve.*
2. Complete your vocabulary assignment for 2 days after the exam.

Examination: *Nectar in a Sieve*

Directions: Select any two of the following questions and answer each in an essay of at least 150 words. Support each answer with as many examples as possible from Markandaya's novel. References to quotations discussed in class will be viewed favorably.

1. Discuss the suffering Rukmani endures because of members of her family.
2. In a society such as Rukmani's, what hope exists for improvement? Should stoicism prevail? Which characters in the book would you say could help India the most? Explain.
3. What does Ira's turning to prostitution suggest about her character? How does her character compare or contrast to her father's?
4. Suggest what you think the family will do to survive now that Rukmani has returned to Selvam at the book's conclusion.
5. Discuss the meaning of the novel's title.

Resource B

Lesson Plans for
Hawthorne's *The Scarlet Letter*

Prepared for an 11th-grade class

The text used for these lessons was *The Scarlet Letter* in Fuller, E., & Achtenhagen, O. (Eds.). (1959). *Four American Novels.* New York: Harcourt, Brace & World.

Aim: What is interesting about reading Hawthorne's *The Scarlet Letter?*
Objective: Pupils will read the first several pages of the *The Scarlet Letter.*

1. Suppose you had grown up in a different place or time—say, the 1960s? What differences might you have found in yourself with regard to
   a. Music
   b. Religion
   c. Clothing styles
   d. School
   e. Politics

2. What would you say is different now from then concerning
   a. People's temperaments
   b. Marriage
   c. Entertainment
   d. Religion
3. Medial summary: We have considered certain differences that existed between now and 30 years ago without even considering having grown up in a different place. We are about to begin a difficult book written by an American named Nathaniel Hawthorne. The book is titled *The Scarlet Letter,* and it deals with people who left England and landed by boat in North America in the early and middle 17th century (1620-1650). That is not 30 but 300 years ago.
4. What were these people called? Do you remember anything about them from your studies in American history? (Probable pupil response will be "Pilgrims.")
5. Teacher may place the word *Puritanism* on the board and inquire if the pupils have any knowledge of the term. The following information might be included on the board:
   a. Protestants who left England because they disagreed with how the church of England was run
   b. Belief that religion should be "pure"—no ceremonies, colored windows, statues, or music
   c. Theocracy: church governs the state
   d. Life on earth is a test to see if you get into Heaven
   e. People must keep busy with fruitful work
   f. Laughter is a symptom of sin
   g. Strict belief in Bible and Ten Commandments
   h. Strict code of behavior and harsh punishments
   i. God is wrathful; mercy is forgotten
6. Teacher reads portion of Jonathan Edwards's (1963) *Sinners in the Hands of an Angry God.* What do you think you would have been like back then?

   This that you have heard is the case of everyone of you that are out of Christ. That world of misery, that lake of burning brimstone, is extended abroad under you. There is the dreadful pit of glowing flames of the wrath of God; there is Hell's wide gaping mouth open; and you have nothing to stand upon, nor anything to take hold of; there is nothing between you and Hell but the air; it is only the power and mere pleasure of God that holds you up. . . .

There are black clouds of God's wrath now hanging directly over your heads, full of the dreadful storm, and big with thunder; and were it not for the restraining hand of God, it would immediately burst forth upon you. The sovereign pleasure of God, for the present, stays His rough wind; otherwise it would come with fury, and your destruction would come like a whirl-wind, and you would be like the chaff of the summer thresh-ing floor. . . .

The God that holds you over the pit of Hell, much as one holds a spider, or some other loathsome insect over the fire, abhors you, and is dreadfully provoked. His wrath towards you burns like fire. . . .

Edwards in Fuller &
Klinnick, 1963, p. 435

7. *The Scarlet Letter,* by Hawthorne, is written in difficult, formal lan-guage. You will be asked to make a list of words that you do not understand as you read. The teacher places the word, *Characters,* on the board and places underneath it:
   a. Hester Prynne: adulteress
   b. Dimmesdale: town minister
   c. Chillingworth: doctor with secret identity
   d. Pearl: Hester's child

The story deals with sin and punishment. It will be up to us to determine who creates the greatest sin. "Who creates the greatest sin?" may be written on the board.

8. Teacher distributes books and receipts. Pupils may begin to read the first several pages.

Homework

1. Read pages 34 through 42 of *The Scarlet Letter.*
2. Record three lines from Chapter 1 that describe the jail.
3. Record three lines from Chapter 2 that show the anger of the women in the town.
4. List 10 unfamiliar vocabulary words.

Aim: How does Hawthorne set the story's mood with his description of the jail and the women's anger?

Objective: Pupils will write a paragraph about the harshness of the Puritan town.

1. The other day we learned a new word—*theocracy*. What is it? (State governed by church) What was the religion of the Puritan people? (Christianity)
2. What is a major principle of Christianity? Teacher writes on board: A major principle of Christianity is forgiveness or mercy.
3. But the first chapter of *The Scarlet Letter* doesn't describe a church. What does it describe? Why is it necessary to have a prison in town? What does it suggest, especially considering it is the oldest building in the town?
4. Describe the prison with lines you recorded for your homework from the text. Teacher writes on board:

The Prison

   a. "Marked with weatherstains" (p. 34)
   b. "Beetlebrowed and gloomy" (p. 34)
   c. "Rust on ponderous iron-work" (p. 34)
   d. "Ugly edifice" (p. 34)
   e. "Unsightly vegetation" (p. 34)
   f. "Black flower of civilized world" (p. 35)

(These are some of the lines that pupils should have recorded for their homework. They will probably need additional explanation from other pupils and the teacher.)

5. Medial summary: Why is it ironic that in a Christian society one of the first buildings built was a prison?
6. In Chapter 2, a woman is led out of the prison to parade herself in front of the townspeople as part of her punishment. What had she done?
7. How does the town react, especially the women? Individuals may be called on to read some or all of the following lines appearing on page 37 of the text:
   a. "Goodwives . . ."
   b. "People say . . ."
   c. "The magistrates . . ."
   d. "This woman has brought shame . . ."

8. Why are the women so harsh? What do they criticize so strongly?
9. Teacher reads from page 8: "The young woman . . ." to page 9, ". . . in a sphere by herself."
10. What is Hester's remaining punishment? What is your opinion of it?
11. Write a paragraph about what you've learned about the town thus far. Teacher circulates and examines pupil writing.

Homework

1. Read Chapters 3 and 4 (pp. 43-55) of *The Scarlet Letter.*
2. Answer the following:
   a. Record the line that shows Hester's refusal to name the father of her child. (pp. 48-49) Is Hester right not to name him?
   b. Who is Chillingworth? What does he ask of Hester? Should she keep her promise to him? Why?
3. Record 10 vocabulary words you do not know.

Aim: How does Hawthorne complicate Hester's life in Chapters 3 and 4?

Objective: Pupils will record notes from reports given by their peers on issues arising in Chapters 3 and 4 of *The Scarlet Letter.*

1. For a story to retain people's interest, it must involve more than everyday, routine life. The story must involve human struggles and complications.
2. What have we learned about the story so far?
3. On pages 48 and 49, what additional complication occurs? (Hester refuses to reveal the identity of her child's father.) A pupil reads the lines from the text.
4. Pages 53 and 55 reveal more. What happens? (Chillingworth, an older man, is Hester's husband, who had not been around for 7 years because he had been kidnapped by Indians. Hester promises not to reveal his identity.) Pupil reads lines from the text.
5. Medial summary: These complications bring out several issues that you need to consider. Teacher establishes four groups at random. A recorder and spokesperson must be selected for each group.
6. Groups are given 10 minutes to record opinions and reasons for the following:
   a. Hester's refusal to reveal the identity of her child's father
   b. Chillingworth's anger at Hester's betrayal
   c. Hester's promise to keep Chillingworth's identity secret
   d. The child's father's failure to reveal himself

(The spokesperson must be instructed to speak slowly and clearly, focusing on people's reasons for opinions, so peers can take notes.)

7. Pupils report while class takes notes. Oral reactions from peers are both permissible and desirable.

Homework

1. Read Chapters 5 and 6 (pp. 55-69) of *The Scarlet Letter.*
2. Answer the following:
   a. Record the lines (pp. 58-60) that show how Hester makes a living.
   b. Record three lines that indicate Pearl's characteristics. (pp. 63-68)
3. Record 10 vocabulary words you do not know.

Aim: How might we use 10 of Hawthorne's vocabulary words from Chapters 1 through 4 of *The Scarlet Letter* in our own sentences?

Objective: Pupils will create and record 10 original sentences that use words taken from Chapters 1 through 4 of *The Scarlet Letter.*

1. *The Scarlet Letter* has too many unfamiliar words for us to study and learn in one semester, but we should try to learn some. You have been asked to list words you do not know in each of your homework assignments. I am going to read a list of words I have made from the first four chapters of *The Scarlet Letter*. The 10 words that have been selected by most of you will be the ones we will study together.

2. The teacher reads the following list of words:

   Chapter 1: throng, ponderous, edifice, vegetation

   Chapter 2: grim, rigidity, culprit, tribunal, scourge, idle, vagrant, magistrate, venerable, infliction, penal, impropriety, interpose, hussy, dismal, beadle, repel, impulse, abashed, exquisite, brazen, apparel, rheumatic, visage, rankle, pillory, ignominy, prone, attire, tread, repress, infer, intolerable, countenance, conspicuous, spectral, obliterate, cloister, intricate

   Chapter 3: manifest, writhing, keen, penetrative, redeem, sojourn, grievous, irk, pedestal, infamy, solemn, append, eminent, virtuous, err, vile, purport, exhort, eloquence, tremulous, trod, compel, plaintive, vacant, stern, discourse, indifference, remorseless, ordeal

   Chapter 4: insubordination, rebuke, quell, intimated, mingle, alchemy, bestow, scrutiny, requited, epoch, bliss

(After approximately 10 minutes, the following words were selected by my class: tribunal, magistrate, impropriety, grievous, stern, insubordination, redeem, infamy, remorseless, rankle.)

3. Teacher forms class into five groups at random, each group responsible for defining two words, finding the sentences in the text in which they appear, and creating an original sentence for each word. A dictionary should be available for each group. Teacher circulates to assist.

4. A member from each group places the words, definitions, and original pupil-constructed sentences on the board for class scrutiny and note taking. Teacher and pupils may make improvements on the boardwork if necessary.

Homework

1. Yesterday's assignment is due.
2. A full-period test will be given after we complete discussion of Chapter 6.

Aim: What consequences did Hester suffer for bearing a child out of wedlock?

Objective: Pupils will write a paragraph about Hester's difficulties as an unwed mother.

1. Today we have far more people being born to mothers who are not married. What problems exist today for an unmarried woman who has a child? (lack of money, child rearing with no male role model, stigma, inability to achieve personal goals)
2. What differences exist between the Puritan outlook on unwed mothers and today's American outlook in New York City?
3. Medial summary: We can see that even in 20th-century America single women with children do not have it easy. But in Hester Prynne's time, things were much worse for an unmarried woman with a child.
4. How did Hester earn a living? (nursing people, needlework)
5. What and for whom does Hester sew? (pp. 42-44) Teacher writes on board:

Hester's Sewing

   a. Ruffs
   b. Bands
   c. Gloves
   d. Funeral attire
   e. Military attire
   f. Minister's attire

6. What is Hester never asked to sew and why? (bridal work)
7. What problems is Hester having raising Pearl?
8. What significance is there in the child's name, Pearl? (p. 62)
9. What kind of a child is Pearl? (pp. 62-64) Pupils are required to respond from their homework. Teacher writes on board:

Pearl

   a. Physically beautiful
   b. Flighty (variety of moods)
   c. Defiant (breaks rules)
   d. Active
   e. Loner (doesn't play with other children)

10. Is Pearl an "imp of evil" or an "emblem of sin?" Read pages 65 and 66 to help you answer.

11. Write a paragraph that discusses the problems Hester had as an unwed mother. Teacher circulates to assist with pupil writing.

Homework

1. Read Chapters 7 and 8 (pp. 70-82) of *The Scarlet Letter.*
2. Answer the following:
   a. List three characteristics of the governor's house. (pp. 72-74)
   b. How does Dimmesdale help Hester in Chapter 8? Why does he do it? (pp. 79-81)
3. List 10 vocabulary words you do not know.

Test: Chapters 1
Through 6 of *The Scarlet Letter*

Vocabulary (25 points): Choose any 5 of the 10 words listed next and write either a definition or a sentence that shows you know the meaning for each: magistrate, impropriety, ignominy, redeem, grievous, stern, tribunal, infamy, remorseless, rankle.

Short answers (50 points): Answer each question in as few words as possible.

1. What two structures did the Puritans build first in their new town?
2. Why was a large crowd gathered at the marketplace?
3. How did most of the town's women regard Hester's punishment?
4. Who is the stranger who appears with an Indian?
5. What promise does Hester make to her husband?
6. How does Hester earn money?
7. What is the only ornament Hester wears around her neck?
8. Why does Hester name her child Pearl?
9. Describe Pearl's nature.
10. With whom did Pearl usually play?

Essay (25 points): In a paragraph of approximately 75 to 100 words describe Hester's punishment by the community and discuss your opinion of its appropriateness.

Aim: Why are parents usually very attached to their children?

Objective: Pupils will write a reaction to Hester's comment in Chapter 8: "Had they taken her from me . . . with my own blood" (p. 81).

1. Cases have arisen in modern times in which children have been taken from their natural parents. Have you ever heard of such cases? What happened?
2. What institution exists that may take children from their natural parents? Why are courts reluctant to do it?
3. In Chapter 7 Hester is called to the governor's house because it is believed that she may not be fit to care for Pearl. What is the governor's house like? Teacher writes on board:

Governor's House

a. Portraits of forefathers: "sternness," "severity"
b. Suit of mail worn by governor (warrior)
c. Convex mirror (makes things look larger)

(Preceding answers are developed from pupil homework.)

4. Medial summary: Why was Hester summoned? What impression do you have of the governor based on the appearance of his house? What do we anticipate will happen? Will they be sympathetic to Hester?
5. Why does the governor want to take Pearl from Hester?
6. How does Dimmesdale help? What does he say? (pp. 79-81) Do you agree with his reasons?
7. Why does Dimmesdale offer this help?
8. Teacher reads line on page 81. What does Hester mean by this? Write a reaction to it in 25 to 50 words. Teacher circulates to examine and assist pupil writing.

Homework

1. Read Chapters 9 and 10 (pp. 82-97) of *The Scarlet Letter.*
2. Answer the following:
   a. Record two lines that show how people regarded Chillingworth's assistance to Dimmesdale. (pp. 83-85)
   b. Record one line that shows Chillingworth was under some type of suspicion. (p. 91)
   c. What explanation does Dimmesdale give for why it's better for some guilty people not to confess? (p. 95)
3. Record 10 vocabulary words you do not know.

Aim: How might we use 10 of Hawthorne's vocabulary words from Chapters 5 through 8 of *The Scarlet Letter* in our own sentences?

Objective: Pupils will create and record 10 original sentences that use words taken from Chapters 5 through 8 of *The Scarlet Letter.*

1. Same as first vocabulary lesson for *The Scarlet Letter.* Teacher instructs pupils to take out their homework and raise their hands when a word is mentioned that they selected. Those 10 words most commonly chosen will be studied. The process should take approximately 10 minutes.

2. Teacher reads the following list of words:
   Chapter 5: threshold, procession, suffice, fatality, pilgrim, martyrdom, peninsula, denote, sable, ordination, pomp, mortify, penance, revile, anguish, throb, imbibe, callous, pang, insidious, piety, sanctified, matron, avert, sullied, grotesque, aver
   Chapter 6: apprehension, clad, rustic, morbid, imbue, infinite, procure, mutability, amenable, impassioned, rebuke, wholesome, regimen, impose, inexplicable, intangibility, malicious, baffling, convulse, conjuration, incomprehensible, sportive, placidity, inviolable, inalienable, discern, appall, intolerant, brood, manifestation, multitude, melancholy, preternatural, abyss, gesticulation, suppress
   Chapter 7: supposition, ultimate, solitary, luxuriant, wan, pallid, lavish, ingenuity, wayfarer, urchin, dauntless, pestilent, imperative, dusky, stucco, commodity, tankard, convex, prominent, pacified, vista, uncanny, disposition
   Chapter 8: antiquated, utmost, aspect, autumnal, reproof, transgression, ascend, vanity, esteem, plumage, temporal, perversity, inopportune, depravity, proximity, careworn, emaciated, profane, sunder, frailty

(The following words were selected by my class: mortify, imbibe, insidious, placid, dauntless, antiquated, transgression, pacified, emaciated, autumnal.)

3. Five groups are formed, each responsible for defining two words, finding the sentences in the text in which the words are used, and creating an original sentence for each word. A dictionary should be available for each group. Teacher circulates to assist.

4. On completion, one member from each group places the words, definitions, and pupil-constructed sentences on the board for class scrutiny and note taking. Teacher and pupils comment and correct as needed.

Homework

Previous assignment, Chapters 9 and 10, is due.

Aim: What has Chillingworth been doing to Dimmesdale?

Objective: Pupils will write a paragraph in reaction to Chillingworth's treatment of Dimmesdale.

1. What is a leech? Why is it considered so hideous?
2. Why is Chapter 9 titled "The Leech?" What has Chillingworth chosen to do for revenge? What is your opinion of this?
3. Medial summary: How does the word *insidious* fit Chillingworth? Let's see how the community reacted to him.
4. Take out your homework:
    a. How does the community view Chillingworth's relationship to Dimmesdale? (pp. 83-85) Explain the lines in your own words.
    b. What is Chillingworth really trying to do?
    c. Do you see any significance in the name, "Chillingworth"?
    d. Is anyone in the story aware of Chillingworth's real purpose? (pp. 90-91)
    e. Why will no one help?
    f. What reason (p. 95) does Dimmesdale give for a guilty person's failure to confess? Teacher records this answer on the board. Do you agree?
5. Write a 25 to 50 word reaction to this question: What is your opinion of Chillingworth's behavior toward Dimmesdale? Teacher circulates to assist and examine pupil writing.

Homework

1. Read Chapters 11 and 12 (pp. 97-112) of *The Scarlet Letter.*
2. Answer the following:
    a. Record two lines that show Dimmesdale's excellent reputation as a minister. (pp. 99-100)
    b. Record one line that shows how greatly Dimmesdale has been suffering. (pp. 101-102)
    c. Discuss the "big 'A' " in 25 to 50 words. (pp. 107-109)
3. Record 10 vocabulary words you do not know.

Aim: What conflict is Dimmesdale experiencing?

Objective: Pupils will write a paragraph discussing what Dimmesdale should do about his conflict.

1. How many of you believe the expression, "confession is good for the soul?" Why?
2. What reason has Dimmesdale given for not having confessed? Do you accept this reason as his true reason?
3. What is Dimmesdale's reputation in his community? Teacher writes on board:

Dimmesdale's Reputation

a. Intellectual gifts
b. Moral perceptions
c. "Overshadowed fellow clergymen" (p. 98)
d. Eloquent
e. Young girls adored him
f. Old people admired him

(Preceding responses are developed from pupils' previous night's homework.)

4. Medial summary: Based on what we have seen, is Dimmesdale essentially a man of his word?
5. Does the community's impression of him relieve his suffering? Teacher reads page 109 to class. What does this suggest? (Even if he confessed, people wouldn't believe him.)
6. What has Dimmesdale done to try to relieve his guilt? Teacher writes on board:

Dimmesdale's Suffering

a. Beats self with a whip
b. Fasts
c. Keeps vigils
d. Has visions

(Preceding answers are developed from pupils' previous night's homework.)

7. Where does Dimmesdale go in Chapter 12? (scaffold) What does he do there? What does he see?
8. Why won't Dimmesdale marry Hester?
9. Write 25 to 50 words in answer to the following: What should Dimmesdale do to relieve his suffering? Why? Teacher circulates to examine and assist pupil writing.

Homework

1. Read Chapters 13 and 14 (pp. 101-121) of *The Scarlet Letter.*
2. Answer the following:
   a. How has Hester's life improved during the past 7 years? (p. 116)
   b. What does Hester plan at the end of Chapter 13? (p. 116)
   c. What does Chillingworth say has caused him to become so evil? Record the lines. (pp. 119-120)
3. Record 10 vocabulary words you do not know.
4. Study for test on Chapters 7 through 12, plus vocabulary.

Aim: How might we use 10 of Hawthorne's vocabulary words from Chapters 9 through 12 of *The Scarlet Letter* in our own sentences?

Objective: Pupils will create and record 10 original sentences using words taken from Chapters 9 through 12 of *The Scarlet Letter.*

1. Same as previous vocabulary lesson on *The Scarlet Letter.* Teacher instructs pupils to take out their homework and raise their hands when a word is mentioned that they selected. Those 10 words most commonly chosen will be studied. The process takes approximately 10 minutes.
2. Teacher reads the following list of words:

    Chapter 9: appellation, perilous, contagious, vindicate, resolve, cordially, zeal, intricacy, deportment, testimonial, exemplary, fervent, apostle, scrupulous, parochial, supernatural, despondent, flitty, lapse, anthem, sagacity, affinity, unsavory, morsel, commodious, refutation, mutual, meditative

    Chapter 10: ominous, quivered, stealthy, intuition, intrusive, retribution, askance, propagate, adjacent, traversed, enclosure, tenacious, proffer, remorseful, bestow, profound, repose, ecstasy

    Chapter 11: subsequent, external, interior, subtlety, grizzled, implicit, abhorrence, abstruse, lore, thwart, tolerance, eloquence, veneration, celestial, introspection, ethereal, delude, substantial

    Chapter 12: expanse, zenith, sustain, catarrh, defraud, wield, trifled, verge, disclosure, expiation, bandying, lattice, reverberation, radiant, luminary, lurid, patriarch, decorous, awry, askew, tumultuous, torrent, torpid, sheaf, egotism, firmament, contemplative, replete, scurrilous, visionary

(After approximately 10 minutes, the following words were selected by my class: intricacy, exemplary, tremulous, sagacity, sanctity, intrusive, propagate, abstruse, veneration, reverberation.)

3. Teacher forms class into five groups at random, each group responsible for defining two words, finding the sentences in the text in which they appear, and creating an original sentence for each word. A dictionary should be available for each group. Teacher circulates to assist.
4. A member from each group places the words, definitions, and pupil-constructed sentences on the board for class scrutiny and note taking. Teacher and pupils may make improvements on the boardwork when necessary.

Homework

1. Study for examination on Chapters 7 through 12.
2. Read Chapters 13 and 14 as assigned.

Test: Chapters 7 Through 12 of *The Scarlet Letter*

Vocabulary (25 points): Choose any 5 words of the 10 listed next and write either a definition or a sentence that shows you know the word's meaning for each: insidious, imbibe, placid, emaciated, dauntless, sanctity, intrusive, reverberation, exemplary, abstruse.

Short answers (50 points): Answer each in as few words as possible.
1. What does the governor want from Hester?
2. Who helps Hester in the governor's mansion?
3. What did Chillingworth say his profession was?
4. What did Dimmesdale do that showed he was in pain?
5. How did the community of Boston perceive the relationship of Chillingworth and Dimmesdale?
6. What does the expression "Black Man" mean?
7. Why is Chillingworth living with Dimmesdale?
8. Why does Dimmesdale climb the scaffold one night?
9. What suggestion is there about Pearl and Dimmesdale when she asks him to join her and her mother on the scaffold in the morning?
10. Why were Hester and Pearl up so late the night Dimmesdale climbed the scaffold?

Essay (25 points): In a 75- to 100-word paragraph, discuss how Dimmesdale suffers. Do you approve of his behavior? Explain.

Aim: How has Hester's life improved since her punishment?

Objective: Pupils will write a paragraph about Hester's improvements in light of Chillingworth's accusation.

1. Teacher writes aphorism on board: "Time heals all wounds." What does this mean?
2. Turn to page 111. Someone reads the line that shows how much time has passed since Hester was punished by being forced to stand on the scaffold in front of the community.
3. What is your opinion regarding the following line: "Human nature loves more readily than it hates."
4. What lines show how Hester's situation has improved? (pp. 111-120) Teacher writes on board:

How Has Time Treated Hester?

   a. "She was a self-ordained Sister of Mercy." (p. 112)
   b. People said the scarlet "A" meant *able.*
   c. "Society was inclined to show its victim a more friendly countenance." (pp. 112-113)
   d. "Individuals in private life . . . had quite forgiven Hester." (p. 113)
   e. Scarlet letter was perceived as a symbol of her good deeds.
   f. "The scarlet letter had the effect of the cross on a nun's bosom." (p. 113)

(Preceding answers are developed from pupils' previous night's homework.)

5. Medial summary: Are you pleased with what has happened to Hester?
6. Hester still has a major problem. What does she plan to do at the end of Chapter 13? (Pupil reads aloud the lines on p. 116.)
7. Hester has made a promise to Chillingworth. What would you advise her about that promise?
8. What happens when Hester confronts Chillingworth? What does he say? See pages 119 and 120. (Pupil reads Chillingworth's lines aloud.)
9. Write a 25 to 50 word paragraph: Are you pleased with Hester's progress? Why? What should she do about Chillingworth? Teacher circulates to examine and assist pupil writing.

Homework

1. Read Chapters 15 and 16 (pp. 121-131) of *The Scarlet Letter.*
2. Answer the following:
    a. Discuss, in 50 words, your reasons for approving or disapproving of what Hester does in Chapter 15.
    b. What does Hester mean on page 129 when she tells Pearl about "meeting the Black Man once?"
3. List 10 vocabulary words you do not know.

Aim: What should Hester have told Pearl about the scarlet letter?

Objective: Pupils will write a paragraph about what they believe Hester should have told Pearl about the scarlet letter.

1. Do you remember being asked as a child to leave the room because the adults were talking about something they didn't want you to hear? Did they spell certain parts of their conversation when you were there? Why? Do you believe this is sometimes a good thing to do? Should children always be told the truth about things they might not understand?
2. What is Pearl always curious about?
3. Would you say Pearl is a bright child? How do you know? Turn to page 124. Teacher writes on board:

What Has Pearl Observed?

   a. "Ask yonder old man who thou hast been talking with." (p. 124)
   b. "Why does the minister keep his hand over his heart?" (p. 124)
   c. "It is for the same reason that the minister keeps his hand over his heart." (p. 124)
   d. "Why does he not wear it on the outside as thou dost, mother?" (p. 130)

4. Medial summary: What does the expression, "Out of the mouths of babes come words of wisdom" mean? Explain how the line applies to Pearl.
5. On page 124, as smart as Pearl is, Hester lies to her about the scarlet letter. Why?
6. Do you approve of Hester lying to Pearl about *The Scarlet Letter*?
7. Turn to page 130. Read silently. What has Hester done here?
8. Teacher writes on board:

Interpretations of Hester's "Black Man"

   a. The sin of adultery
   b. The error of having married Chillingworth (pp. 128-129)
   c. The sin of extreme punishment by the town

9. Write a paragraph of 25 to 50 words about whether Hester was wise in the way she explained *The Scarlet Letter* to Pearl? Would you do things differently if you were a parent? Teacher circulates to examine and assist pupil writing.

Homework

1. Read Chapters 17 and 18 (pp. 131-141) of *The Scarlet Letter.*
2. Answer the following:
   a. What does Hester mean when she tells Dimmesdale "Thou shalt not go alone." (pp. 137-138)
   b. After completing Chapter 18, write 25 to 50 words on how you believe the story will end.
3. List 10 vocabulary words you do not know.

Aim: How might we use 10 of Hawthorne's vocabulary words from Chapters 13 through 16 of *The Scarlet Letter* in our own sentences?

Objective: Pupils will create and record 10 original sentences using words taken from Chapters 13 through 16 of *The Scarlet Letter.*

1. Same as last vocabulary lesson on *The Scarlet Letter.* Teacher instructs pupils to take out their homework and raise their hands when a word is mentioned that they selected. The 10 words most commonly chosen will be studied. The process takes approximately 5 minutes.
2. Teacher reads the following list of words:
   Chapter 13: abase, grovel, seclusion, pauper, gibe, despotic, benevolence, transfiguration, speculate, prophetess, wreak, venom, guise
   Chapter 14: entreaty, derisive, vigor, gloat, extort, perpetration, despair, perpetual, direst, usurp, implore, dismal
   Chapter 15: verdure, earnestness
   Chapter 16: untransmitted, vivacity

(After approximately 5 minutes, the following words were selected by my class: abase, seclusion, despotic, speculate, derisive, gloat, perpetual, usurp, reciprocate, vivacity.)

3. Teacher forms class into five groups at random, each group responsible for defining two words, finding the sentences in the text in which they appear, and creating an original sentence for each word. A dictionary should be available for each group. Teacher circulates to assist.
4. A member of each group places the words, definitions, and pupil-constructed sentences on the board for class scrutiny and note taking. Teacher and pupils may make improvements of the boardwork when necessary.

Homework

Read Chapters 17 and 18 as previously assigned.

Aim: What is your opinion of the love shared by Hester and Dimmesdale?
Objective: Based on homework and discussion, pupils will write a paragraph that furthers their predictions about the conclusion to *The Scarlet Letter.*

1. Teacher reads line on page 133: ". . . Arthur Dimmesdale put forth his hand, chill as death, and touched the chill hand of Hester Prynne." What are these people feeling? What do you think each one is thinking? Explain your answers.
2. Do you believe these two love each other? What lines suggest they do? (pp. 133-135) Teacher writes on board:

Love Between Hester and Dimmesdale

a. "You wrong yourself in this . . ." (p. 133)
b. "Such a friend . . . you have in me." (p. 133)
c. Hester reveals Chillingworth's identity (p. 134)
d. "Thou shalt forgive . . ." (p. 135)
e. "What we did had a consecration . . . . We said so." (p. 135)
f. "No, I have not forgotten." (p. 135)

(The preceding answers are derived by announcing the page number and asking the pupils to examine the page for a line suggesting a love relationship between Hester and Dimmesdale.)

3. Look at your homework. What does Hester mean when she says, "Thou shalt not go alone?" Why is he so afraid of being alone?
4. Medial summary: Apparently, based on their characters and on what they say to each other, Hester and Dimmesdale do love one another. What are they both overlooking?
5. Chapter 18 is devoted to Pearl. How do we expect she will act on learning that Dimmesdale is her father and they are about to move? Read pages 141 and 142.
6. What line on page 142 enables you to guess what might happen? (last line of page)
7. Read some of your predictions for the story's conclusion.
8. Write more of what you believe will happen at the story's conclusion. Give reasons for your predictions.

Homework

1. Read Chapters 19 and 20 (pp. 142-156).

2. Answer the following:
   a. Was Pearl's behavior in this chapter what you expected? If yes, explain. If no, what did you expect? Why?
   b. How has Dimmesdale changed since his last meeting with Hester? (pp. 149, 154)
3. List 10 vocabulary words you do not know.
4. Study for test on Chapters 13 through 18, plus vocabulary.

Test: Chapters 13
Through 18 of *The Scarlet Letter*

Vocabulary (25 points): Choose any 5 of the 10 words listed next and write either a definition or a sentence that shows you know the word's meaning for each: abase, seclusion, despotic, speculate, derisive, gloat, perpetual, usurp, reciprocate, vivacity.

Short answers (50 points): Answer each in as few words as possible.

1. How many years pass from the beginning of the story to the point that Hester decides to meet Chillingworth in private a second time?
2. What positive word do some people now believe *The Scarlet Letter* stands for?
3. What else does Hester do in the community in addition to needle-work?
4. What does Hester tell Chillingworth?
5. What does Hester want Chillingworth to do?
6. About what does Hester lie to Pearl?
7. Where does Hester choose to meet Dimmesdale?
8. What does Hester reveal to Dimmesdale?
9. What has Dimmesdale both feared and longed for?
10. Why does Dimmesdale say he can't leave Boston?

Essay (25 points): In 75 to 100 words, discuss Chillingworth's plan of vengeance. Do you approve of what he did? Why? If you do not approve, what should he have done? Why?

Aim: How does Pearl's behavior help reveal what will occur at the book's conclusion?

Objective: Students will write a paragraph stating whether they believe Dimmesdale will escape to Europe with Hester.

1. Fairy tales often end "happily ever after." How many of you believe *The Scarlet Letter* will end that way? What is there in the text that supports your feelings?
2. Did Pearl's behavior toward Dimmesdale come as a surprise to you? How did you originally expect her to behave when Hester first called her to Dimmesdale?
3. How did Pearl behave? Turn to your homework (pp. 144-183). Teacher writes on board:

Pearl's Behavior

a. "How slow thou art . . ." (p. 144)
b. "Pearl, without responding . . . remained . . ." (p. 144)
c. "Pearl pointed with her finger." (p. 145)
d. "A frown gathered on her brow." (p. 145)
e. "The child stamped her foot with a yet more imperious look." (p. 179)
f. "But into a fit of passion, gesticulating violently and throwing her small figure . . ." (p. 179)
g. ". . . piercing shrieks . . ." (p. 145)
h. "Pearl put up her mouth and kissed *The Scarlet Letter* too." (p. 145)
i. "Will he go back with us hand in hand . . ." (p. 147)
j. "Pearl broke away . . . the unwelcomed kiss was quite washed off." (p. 147)

(The preceding answers are developed from the text and pupil homework.)

4. Medial summary: How do you feel about Pearl for behaving this way? What do you feel for Dimmesdale?
5. Even though Pearl treats him badly, Dimmesdale seems to have some hope now. What have he and Hester planned?
6. What changes in Dimmesdale's behavior can we see? (p. 149—excitement in his feelings; p. 150—incited to do some wicked thing; p. 154—rejects Chillingworth.) Pupils use their homework to develop answers.

7. Write a 25- to 50-word paragraph on whether you believe Dimmesdale, Hester, and Pearl will lead a new, good life in England. Teacher circulates to examine and assist pupil writing.

Homework

1. Read Chapters 21 and 22 (pp. 155-170).
2. Answer the following:
   a. How does Chillingworth guess Dimmesdale's plan?
   b. Why is it good for the protagonists that on the day they want to run away, there is a big celebration for election day?
3. List 10 vocabulary words you do not know.

Aim: How might we use 10 of Hawthorne's vocabulary words from Chapters 17 through 20 of *The Scarlet Letter* in our own sentences?

Objective: Pupils will create and record 10 original sentences using words taken from Chapters 17 through 20 of *The Scarlet Letter.*

1. Same as last vocabulary lesson on *The Scarlet Letter.* Teacher instructs pupils to take out their homework and raise their hands when a word is mentioned that they selected. The 10 words most commonly chosen will be studied. The process takes approximately 10 minutes.
2. Teacher reads the following list of words.

   Chapter 17: consolation, polluted, malignity, enfeebled, consecration

   Chapter 18: machination, inscrutable, breach, irrevocably, transmuting, breadth, subjugated, illumined, inquisitively, clergyman

   Chapter 19: prattle, picturesque, adornment, foliage, estrange, imperious, extravagant, contortion, pacify, pallor, withering, exertion, reluctance, grimace, diffused

   Chapter 20: solace, vexed, duplicity, disquietude, acute, phenomenon, dell, incite, blasphemous, condense, blight, potent, imperative, purport, sovereign, perverted, eccentricity, tapestried, borne, devoid, tarry, impulsive, tract, bedazzled

(After approximately 10 minutes, my class selected the following words: malignity, polluted, inscrutable, irrevocable, inquisitive, grimace, vex, blasphemous, eccentricity, devoid.)

3. Teacher forms class into five groups at random, each group responsible for defining two words, finding the sentences in the text in which they appear, and creating an original sentence for each word. A dictionary should be available for each group. Teacher circulates to assist.
4. A member of each group places the words, definitions and pupil-constructed sentences on the board for class scrutiny and note taking. Teacher and pupils may make improvements on the boardwork when necessary.

Homework

Read Chapters 21 and 22 as previously assigned.

Aim: What tension does Hawthorne create as we reach the conclusion of *The Scarlet Letter?*

Objective: Pupils will write a summary of the scene in which Hester plans her escape.

1. If a person plans to sneak away with no one knowing, is it better to do it when no one is around or when a celebration with a big crowd is occurring? Explain.
2. What celebration is occurring in Chapter 21?
3. Who is in the marketplace? Read pages 159 through 161. Teacher writes on board:

The Marketplace

   a. Puritans
   b. Indians
   c. Mariners

(Teacher should note with pupils the contrast of the different types of people there.)

4. Medial summary: What has Hawthorne done to make Hester's getaway easier?
5. Teacher reads dialogue on page 162. What does Hester learn from this dialogue?
6. How did Chillingworth learn of Hester's plan to escape? Pupils read from homework.
7. Teacher reads page 165. How did Dimmesdale seem after his sermon?
8. Pupils read page 168. What does Hester realize?
9. Pupils read pages 169 and 170. What has happened to Hester that makes her escape to Europe nearly impossible?
10. Write a paragraph that summarizes how Hawthorne complicated Hester's escape.

Homework

1. Read Chapters 23 and 24 (pp. 171-182).
2. Answer the following:
   a. Copy the last words Dimmesdale says to Chillingworth (top of p. 176) and to Hester (bottom of p. 176 to top of p. 178). Explain their significance.

    b. What happens in the final chapter? Does the ending satisfy you? How would you have ended the story?

3. List 10 vocabulary words you do not know.

Aim: What is the main idea in Hawthorne's *The Scarlet Letter?*

Objective: Pupils will write a paragraph expressing the reason for the book's tragic conclusion (sin of hypocrisy).

1. Teacher writes on board:

   He that is without sin among you, let him cast a stone at her. Go and sin no more.

   (Jesus Christ, in John 8:7, John 8:11)

   Who said this? What does it mean?

2. In *The Scarlet Letter* we see a good deal of sin. Teacher writes on board:

   ### Sin *in* The Scarlet Letter

   a. Hester's adultery
   b. Dimmesdale's adultery and failure to admit guilt
   c. Chillingworth's vengeance
   d. Community's vengeance on Hester

Preceding answers are derived from pupils through questions such as, "What sin did Hester commit?"

3. In your opinion, which sin is the worst? In what ways were the Puritans hypocrites?

4. Medial summary: South African Alan Paton once said (teacher writes on board),

   [Prison] reforms [are] within the framework of custody, and leave out the importance of freedom and responsibility as the supreme reformatory instruments.

   Paton, in Callan, 1968, p. 24.

5. Which sin would Alan Paton have said was the worst? Why?

6. If the community had practiced mercy instead of punishment, could the ending have been happier?

7. Dimmesdale has disappointed us in general. How does he redeem himself in the end? Take out your homework.

   a. How does Dimmesdale respond to Chillingworth?
   b. How does Dimmesdale respond to Hester?

8. On page 176, Pearl kisses Dimmesdale. Why has her attitude toward him changed?

9. What do we learn in the final chapter? Teacher writes on board:

The Final Chapter

a. Hester returned to Boston (p. 10)
b. Pearl is married (p. 181)
c. Scarlet letter is no longer a stigma (p. 184)
d. Hester is buried next to Dimmesdale (p. 181)
e. Hester's tombstone has the letter "A" on it.

Preceding answers are derived through use of pupil homework.

10. Write a paragraph that explains how the harshness of the Puritan people caused the sad results of this story.

Aim: How might we use 10 of Hawthorne's vocabulary words from Chapters 21 through 24 of *The Scarlet Letter* in our own sentences?

Objective: Pupils will create and record 10 original sentences using words taken from Chapters 21 through 24 of *The Scarlet Letter.*

1. Same as last vocabulary lesson on *The Scarlet Letter.* Teacher instructs pupils to take out their homework and raise their hands when a word is mentioned that they selected. Those 10 words most commonly chosen will be studied. The process takes approximately 10 minutes.
2. Teacher reads the following list of words:
   Chapter 21: inhabitant, metropolis, apparition, contrive, effluence, hue, procession, jollity, compressed, mirth, affliction, pageantry, commonwealth, grim, interred, posterity, visage, diversity, scruple, arraigned, tempestuous, relinquish, gallant, vessel, incurring, mariner, berth, steward, convoy, remote
   Chapter 22: agitation, inducement, feebleness, exhilaration, cordial, ascend, marshall, steadfast, solitude, intangible, array, garland, auditor, pathos, medium, orb, undulate, indefatigable, minutest, swarthy, smitten, harassed, perplexity, centrifugal, repugnance, languid, surmise
   Chapter 23: aloft, oracle, ensue, tumult, gush, rapture, exalt, clangor, irrepressible, wavering, imperceptible, mien, stigma
   Chapter 24: fidelity, bequeath, armorial, herald

(After approximately 10 minutes, my class selected the following words: fidelity, feebleness, intangible, stigma, tempestuous, swarthy, array, gallant, repugnance, hue.)

3. Five groups are formed, each responsible for defining two words, locating the sentences in the text where they appear, and creating a sentence for each word. A dictionary should be available for each group. Teacher circulates to assist.
4. A member of each group places the words, definitions, and pupil-constructed sentences on the board for class scrutiny and note taking. Teacher and pupils may make improvements of the boardwork when necessary.

Homework

Study for test on Chapters 21 and 24, plus vocabulary.

Test: Chapters 21
Through 24 of *The Scarlet Letter*

Vocabulary (25 points): Choose any 5 of the 10 words listed next and write either a definition or a sentence that shows you know the word's meaning for each: polluted, irrevocable, vex, inquisitive, surmise, tempestuous, intangible, feebleness, stigma, fidelity.

Short answers: (50 points) Answer each question in as few words as possible.

1. Why doesn't Pearl come to Hester and Dimmesdale when her mother calls her?
2. What does Pearl do when Dimmesdale kisses her?
3. What does Pearl expect Dimmesdale to do?
4. Where do Hester and Dimmesdale plan to go?
5. What has caused a procession in Boston?
6. What does Hester learn about her voyage on the ship?
7. How is Dimmesdale regarded by the people of the town?
8. Where is Dimmesdale when he says his final words
9. To whom does Chillingworth leave property?
10. What finally happens to Hester?

Essay (25 points): Discuss the following statement in approximately 100 words. The greatest sin in the book was committed by the townspeople. (You should consider what happened to all the major characters because of the town's hypocrisy.)

Resource C

Lesson Plans for Shakespeare's *Macbeth*

Prepared for a 12th-grade class above grade level

The text used for these lessons was Wright, L. B., & LaMar, V. (Eds.). (1959). *Macbeth.* New York: Simon & Schuster.

Aim: Why do high school students around the world study Shakespearean plays?

Objective: Pupils will orally interpret Shakespearean lines.

1. What Shakespearean plays have you read or seen? What were the stories about? Where did you see them? Did you like them?
2. Is there anything you did not like about Shakespeare?
3. To explain Shakespearean language, the teacher asks a series of questions, makes comments, and offers examples from the text of *Macbeth.*
   a. Why is the language so very different? (The language is from 17th-century England, not 20th-century America.)

    b. Examine the following sentence and explain why a person living in New York 100 years from now might have difficulty interpreting it even with the help of a dictionary: "Let's split to my crib and get stoned."

    c. Shakespeare's dialogue is written in poetry including rich imagery and meter.

4. Listen to and interpret the following lines:

    a. Lennox: Who cannot want the thought how monstrous/It was for Malcolm and for Donalbain/To kill their gracious father. (p. 55)

    b. Porter: Yet I made a shift to cast him. (p. 29)

    c. Duncan: There's no art/To find the mind's construction in the face. (p. 11)

    d. Macbeth: For in my way it lies. (p. 18) (Teacher may explain the inverted form of "For it lies in my way" as a method of preserving the rhythm. Iambic pentameter may be explained at this point.)

    e. Macbeth: O, full of scorpions is my mind . . . (p. 44)

    f. Ross: Bellona's bridegroom . . . (p. 4)

5. The teacher should demonstrate the use of the marginal notes on the alternate pages of the Folger Edition of *Macbeth*.

6. Medial summary: Although many American teens complain about Shakespeare's language being difficult for 20th-century Americans, once understood, the language will give these same people additional enjoyment of the play. Why?

7. Despite their language differences, Shakespeare's plays have endured for 400 years for many of the reasons you offered at the beginning of the period. Teacher distributes "The Greatness of Shakespeare" (see p. 134). Pupils read this handout. Is there anything you might want to add at this point?

8. Let's examine some of Shakespeare's lines from his plays and see if we can understand them even out of context. Teacher distributes "Five Shakespearean Quotations" for pupil interpretation (see pp. 134-135). Pupils respond orally to the lines.

Homework

Assume that a psychic says to you, "You will one day achieve everlasting fame and great wealth, doing something you always wanted and deserved." Write 100 words on what you would do about it for the next several months. If the answer is "nothing," explain why in approximately 100 words.

The Greatness of Shakespeare

Greatness in writers is measured in part by the quality and the quantity of their work but mainly by the endurance of their work. Shakespeare's work has lasted a long time—400 years! Relative to other writers of his generation, we should note that Shakespeare was by no means prolific. In fact, he wrote only 37 plays, but each is excellent and all are still staged in various parts of the world in this century. The scope of his work shows almost unbelievable versatility. Unlike Sophocles, who wrote only tragedy, or Aristophanes, who wrote only comedy, Shakespeare wrote both! Furthermore, he also wrote plays on historical figures and events. Here is a partial listing of some of his masterpieces. I'm sure you've heard of several.

Tragedies
  Hamlet
  King Lear
  Othello
  Macbeth
  Julius Caesar
Comedies
  As You Like It
  A Midsummer Night's Dream
  Twelfth Night
  Much Ado About Nothing
  The Taming of the Shrew
Histories
  Richard II
  Richard III
  Henry IV: Part I
  Henry IV: Part II
  Henry V

In addition, Shakespeare's sonnets (14-line love poems), filled with emotion, are considered by most literary scholars to be the most elegant, not only in the English language but in the entire world.

Five Shakespearean Quotations

But soft. What light through yonder window breaks?/It is the east and Juliet is the sun./Arise, fair sun, and kill the envious moon,/Who is already sick and pale with grief/That thou her maid art far more fair than she.

Romeo from Romeo and Juliet, Act II, Scene 2

To be, or not to be. That is the question./Whether 'tis nobler the mind to suffer/The slings and arrows of outrageous fortune/ Or to take arms against a sea of troubles,/And by opposing, end them.

Hamlet from Hamlet, Act III, Scene 2

The evil that men do lives after them./The good is oft interred with their bones./So let it be with Caesar.

Marc Antony from Julius Caesar, Act III, Scene 2

The quality of mercy is not strained,/It droppeth like the gentle rain from heaven,/Upon the place beneath; it is twice blessed;/ It blesseth him that gives and him that takes.

Portia from The Merchant of Venice, Act IV Scene 1

Life's but a walking shadow, a poor player/That struts and frets his hour upon the stage/Then is heard no more; it is a tale/ Told by an idiot, full of sound and fury/Signifying nothing.

Macbeth from Macbeth, Act V, Scene 5

The day after the lesson on Shakespearean language, the teacher distributes a supplementary assignment (see following page).

Aim: What Shakespearean assignment am I best suited to complete?

Objective: Pupils will write a paragraph, to be collected by the teacher, on their choice for a supplementary assignment.

I. Teacher distributes the following assignment:

Honor Class Supplementary Assignment

At the conclusion of our study of *Macbeth* and after we have seen either a stage or film production of it, you will be given 5 minutes to further educate your peers on Shakespearean lore, technique, and so on. A partial list of assignments follows. Should your selection differ from this list, please consult your teacher. In any case, once settled on a topic, consult your teacher to avoid unnecessary duplication with other students. Should your performance involve more than one person, your time limit will expand to 5 minutes per person.

1. Perform a scene from *Macbeth.*
   a. Macbeth and Lady Macbeth: Act I, Scene 7
   b. Macbeth and Lady Macbeth: Act II, Scene 2
   c. Macbeth and Lady Macbeth: Act IV, Scene 3
2. Perform a monologue from *Macbeth.*
   a. "Two truths are told . . ." Act I, Scene 3
   b. Lady Macbeth, Act I, Scene 5
   c. "If it were done . . ." Act I, Scene 7
   d. "Is this a dagger . . ." Act II, Scene 1
   e. Porter, Act II, Scene 3
   f. "To be thus is nothing . . ." Act III, Scene 1
   g. "Tomorrow and tomorrow . . ." Act V, Scene 5
3. Report on the various productions of *Macbeth.*
4. Report on 11th-century Scotland, its wars, economy, culture, traditions, and so forth.
5. Analyze Shakespeare's use of metaphor and rhythm in *Macbeth.*
6. Analyze Shakespeare's use of animals, color, light and dark in a report on the atmosphere in *Macbeth.*
7. Report on *Macbeth* as classical tragedy (see p. 170).
8. Select one of the following issues and debate it:
   a. Lady Macbeth's faint is not real.
   b. Macbeth did not need Lady Macbeth's influence to kill Duncan.
   c. The witches caused Macbeth to kill Duncan.
9. Compare *Macbeth* to another Shakespearean tragedy you have studied, or contrast it to a Shakespearean comedy you have studied.

10. Compare *Macbeth* to a modern tragedy you have studied.
11. Report on performance technique in Shakespeare's day: costuming, scenery, special effects, style of acting.
12. Report on the theaters, especially the Globe, in Shakespeare's day.
13. Report on a biography you read of Shakespeare's life.
14. Write a sequel or a "prequel" to *Macbeth*.
15. Report on Shakespeare's position in the Chamberlain's Company and discuss Elizabeth I's and James I's influence on drama during the era.
16. Report on superstition and belief in the supernatural in both 11th-century Scotland and Shakespeare's England.
17. Analyze how "fair is foul and foul is fair" is a theme that permeates *Macbeth*.
18. Create a newspaper that might have existed in Scotland the day after Duncan's assassination.
19. Defend or prosecute Macbeth on his application to get into Heaven.
20. Create a diary Macbeth might have kept from before he met the witches to the assassination of Macduff's family.
21. Prove that Shakespeare wrote Shakespeare's works.
22. Draw, paint, sculpt, and so forth your depictions of *Macbeth*.

Approximate due date: _____

II. Pupils may ask questions and make suggestions about the assignment.

III. Pupils write a paragraph about selecting a topic. (Their selection may eventually be altered, but there will be a deadline beyond which their choices must remain fixed.) Teacher circulates to assist and correct pupil writing.

IV. Teacher distributes "Partial Bibliography" (see p. 169).

V. Teacher collects paragraphs from pupils.

Partial Bibliography

Shakespeare's Life

Chute, M. (1947). *Shakespeare of London*. New York: E. P. Dutton.
Haliday, F. E. (1956). *Shakespeare: A pictorial biography*. New York: Viking.
Harrison, G. B. (1933). *Shakespeare under Elizabeth*. New York: Henry Holt.
Rowse, A. L. (1963). *William Shakespeare: A biography*. New York: Harper & Row.

Shakespeare's Plays as Theater

Beckerman, B. (1962). *Shakespeare at the Globe: 1599-1609*. New York: Macmillan.
Joseph, B. (1962). *Acting Shakespeare*. London: Routledge & Kegan Paul.
Thorndike, A. H. (1928). *Shakespeare's theater*. New York: Macmillan.
Webster, M. (1942). *Shakespeare without tears*. New York: McGraw-Hill.
Williams, F. (1941). *Mr. Shakespeare at the Globe*. New York: E. P. Dutton.

Criticism

Dowden, E. (1918). *Shakespeare: A critical study of his mind and art*. New York: Harper & Brothers.
Granville-Barker, H., & Harrison, G. B. (Eds.). (1937). *A companion to Shakespeare studies*. New York: Macmillan.
Muir, K., & Schoenbaum, S. (Eds.). (1971). A new companion to Shakespeare studies. Cambridge, UK: Cambridge University Press.
Raysor, T. M. (Ed.). (1962). *Samuel Taylor Coleridge: Shakespeare criticism* (Vols. 1-2). New York: E. P. Dutton.
Sandler, R. (Ed.). (1986). *Northrop Frye on Shakespeare*. New Haven, CT: Yale University Press.
Seigel, P. N. (Ed.). (1964). *His infinite variety*. Philadelphia: J. P. Lippencott.

History

Brown, I. (1963). *How Shakespeare spent the day*. New York: Hill & Wang.
Hosley, R. (Ed.). (1968). *Shakespeare's Holinshed*. New York: G. P. Putnam.
Knight, W. N. (1973). *Shakespeare's hidden life: Shakespeare at the law, 1585-1595*. New York: Mason & Lipscomb.

Ogburn, D., & Ogburn, C., Jr. (1962). *Shakespeare: The man behind the name.* New York: William Morrow.

Reese, M. M. (1953). *Shakespeare: His world and his work.* Suffolk, UK: Richard Clay.

Aim: What can we anticipate in our study of *Macbeth*?
Objective: Pupils will write suggestions for opening scenes to *Macbeth*.

1. Teacher places following line on the board and asks for pupil interpretation.

   There are those who are ruled by destiny and there are those who take destiny by the hand.

2. Take out your homework. Read aloud your reaction to the "psychic" who predicted your good fortune. Is there anyone who implied that he or she would do "anything" to reach the goal? Why?
3. Medial summary: What adjectives would you apply, and why, to the person who is led by destiny? To the person who takes destiny by the hand?
4. *Macbeth* is a play based on the concept of fate and free will. Teacher writes on the board:

Macbeth

   a. Place: Scotland
   b. Time: 11th century
   c. Atmosphere: Civil war and war against Norway
   d. Plot: Great Scottish warrior is told by supernatural characters that he will become king
   e. Characters
      Macbeth: Nobleman, warrior
      Lady Macbeth: Devoted wife
      Banquo: Nobleman, warrior, friend to Macbeth
      Duncan: King of Scotland
      Malcolm: Son of Duncan, heir to the throne
      Donalbain: Younger son of Duncan
      Macduff: Nobleman, warrior
   f. Elements
      Heroism
      War and bloodshed
      Conscience
      Supernatural
      Tragedy: The fall of a great man
      Fate versus free will

5. Knowing this much about the play, what should a dramatist do to create attention in the opening scene? Write such an opening scene.
6. Pupils are called on to read scenes aloud.
7. Teacher distributes books and book receipts.

Homework

1. Read Act I, Scenes 1 and 2.
2. Answer the following:
   a. Do you approve of the opening scene? How could you add 5 minutes of motivating action to it?
   b. What do we learn about Macbeth in Scene 2? Record the lines that discuss his abilities.
3. Define: valor, direful, dispersed, deign, minion.

Aim: How did Shakespeare "advertise" a showdown between the witches and Macbeth in the opening scenes of Macbeth?

Objective: Pupils will write a paragraph about what they anticipate happening when the witches meet Macbeth.

1. Teacher reads the opening scene, which takes approximately 10 seconds. Considering that an opening scene is meant, in part, to capture attention, Shakespeare seems to have not realized this need. But we already know he is one of the best playwrights who ever lived. Therefore, we must assume he knew otherwise. What did you say in your homework about the opening scene?
2. Teacher writes on board:

First Scene *of* Macbeth

    a. Atmosphere—Fog, storm
    b. War, battle scene
    c. Witches

3. Describe the witches. What, if anything, seems awesome about their behavior? Teacher elicits and writes on board:

Witches

    a. Appear in horrible weather; may actually control it
    b. Have an appointment with Macbeth
    c. Speak in perverted, twisted language

4. In Shakespeare's time, people had much greater belief in the supernatural. Why is that logical? How would the opening scene, therefore, affect an Elizabethan audience?
5. With regard to the witches' language, what lines suggest impossible situations that can still be explained? These lines are called *paradoxes*. Teacher places the word and its definition on the board: Paradox—an expression that contradicts itself yet can be logically explained
6. Please note, as you continue to read *Macbeth*, how frequently what seems good is bad and what seems bad is good. Which line in the opening scene suggests that?
7. What is the one overpowering feeling we have about the witches after viewing this first scene? (fear)

8. What kind of individual could do battle with these witches—Superman, Batman, Indiana Jones? What did you learn about Macbeth from last night's reading?

9. Teacher reads Act I, Scene 2 and asks the following questions:
   a. Who is Macdonald? How does he show Macbeth to his best advantage?
   b. Who is Duncan's army fighting?
   c. What reward is Duncan going to give Macbeth?
   d. Why does this scene and the previous one end in a rhyme?

10. Write a paragraph about what you believe will happen when the great, fearless soldier meets the supernatural witches. Teacher circulates to assist and examine pupil writing. Pupils may read paragraphs aloud, if time permits.

Homework

1. Read Act I, Scene 3.
2. Answer the following:
   a. What prophecies do the witches make for Macbeth? What lines show his reactions?
   b. What prophecies do the witches make for Banquo? What lines show his reactions?
   c. What happens in the scene's end that astounds both men? Why does it astound them?

3. Define: rapt, trifle, surmise, interim.

Aim: What do we learn about Macbeth's inner ambitions?

Objective: Pupils will write a paragraph explaining the difference between Macbeth's and Banquo's reactions to the witches' predictions. Lines from the play must be quoted in these paragraphs.

1. What mythological works have you read that depict battles between superheroes? What about *The Iliad* and *The Odyssey?*
2. What happens during the meeting between the witches and Macbeth? Is it what you anticipated?
3. What prophecies are made to Macbeth, to Banquo?
   Teacher writes on board:

The Witches' Prophecies

To Macbeth
a. He will be Thane of Cawdor
b. He will be king

To Banquo
a. Lesser than Macbeth but greater
b. Not as happy as Macbeth but happier
c. He will "get" kings though he be none

4. Note the types of statements made to Banquo. What are they? (paradoxes) How might they come true?
5. Medial summary: Think back to one of your first assignments on *Macbeth.* How would you react after hearing such predictions?
6. We need now to examine how Macbeth and Banquo reacted. Teacher reads Act I, Scene 3 and asks the following questions:
   a. Why are the witches' words in rhymes? What more do we learn about them?
   b. What does Macbeth mean by, "So foul and fair a day I have not seen"?
   c. Describe the witches' physical appearance.
   d. What is the "insane root"?
   e. What does Banquo mean: "Good sir, why do you start . . ."?
   f. Does Banquo seem as serious as Macbeth?
   g. How do we know that the witches are not figments of Macbeth's imagination?
   h. What news is brought to Macbeth and Banquo that shocks them?
   i. What does Macbeth say to himself in the asides?

j. What feelings does Macbeth display in his "supernatural solicit-ings" speech?

k. How does this differ from Banquo's "Look how our partner's rapt"?

l. What does "If chance will have me King, why chance may crown me" mean?

7. Using lines from the play, discuss the difference between Macbeth's and Banquo's reactions to the witches. Teacher circulates to assist and examine pupil writing. Pupils read responses aloud, if time permits.

Homework

1. Read Act I, Scene 4.
2. Answer the following:
   a. What do we learn about Macbeth's relationship to Duncan?
   b. What important step does Duncan take?
   c. How does Macbeth react publicly and privately to that step?
3. Define: recompense, harbinger.

Aim: What happens to cause Macbeth to think further about the witches' predictions?

Objective: Pupils will discuss orally whether Macbeth will take steps to become king.

1. Our knowledge of succession to a throne tells us that a son or daughter is next in line to rule a country on the death of the present king or queen. But on page ix of the Folger text, the editor states, "He (Macbeth) is near of kin to the King and under the laws of Scotland, he may be chosen to succeed Duncan."

2. By way of review, what do we know of Macbeth's ambitions? How does he feel about these ambitions? (He feels guilt, e.g., the asides.)

3. In Act I, Scene 4, the place shifts to Duncan's castle. What has occurred?

4. What does Malcolm mean by, "Nothing in his life became him like the leaving it"?

5. Discuss Duncan's line, "There's no art/To find the mind's construction in the face./He was a gentleman on whom I built/An absolute trust."

6. What error has Duncan made recently? How does this advance the "fair is foul and foul is fair" theme?

7. Medial summary: Write a 50-word paragraph based on what we've analyzed to date on what you expect Macbeth to do. Teacher circulates to assist and examine pupil writing. Paragraphs are read aloud.

8. What does Duncan do that causes Macbeth to reconsider? (Malcolm is made heir to the throne.)

9. What does Macbeth mean when he says, "The Prince of Cumberland! That is a step/On which I must fall down, or else o'erstep,/For in my way it lies. Stars, hide your fires!/Let not light see my black and deep desires./The eye wink at the hand: yet let that be,/Which the eye fears, when it is done to see"?

10. What do you believe Macbeth will do next, based on what we've analyzed to date? (Pupils must react to previous statements of peers before offering their own.)

Homework

1. Read Act I, Scene 5.
2. Answer the following:
   a. What does Macbeth's letter imply about his relationship with Lady Macbeth?

     b. Record lines that show Lady Macbeth has great respect and love for Macbeth.

     c. Paraphrase Lady Macbeth's prayer to the devil.

     d. What does Lady Macbeth mean by, "O, never/Shall sun that morrow see"?

  3. Define: chastise, impede, dunnest.

Aim: What are your impressions of Lady Macbeth after this scene?

Objective: Pupils will write a paragraph, quoting lines from the scene, that offers their impressions of Lady Macbeth.

1. What is unquestioning admiration and love in a marriage? If your boyfriend or girlfriend told you of an opportunity he or she had to commit a "perfect" crime to get ahead, what would you advise, especially believing the person deserved to get ahead?

2. In last night's homework, what did you determine about Macbeth's relationship with his wife? Teacher writes on board:

Relationship of Macbeth and Lady Macbeth

a. He writes to her so she will share in his joy
b. He wants the title for her
c. He uses terms of equality and endearment
d. She believes he is entitled to be king
e. She respects his honesty; she thinks he is good

(Preceding answers are elicited from pupil homework and lines from the scene under study.)

3. Medial summary: Why does Macbeth give Lady Macbeth this information? What does he expect of her? What will she do for him?

4. On page 15, Lady Macbeth offers a type of prayer. What does she ask for? Read what you paraphrased. (Several pupils may be called on to read.)

5. Teacher reads the "anti-prayer" and asks the following questions:
   a. Why doe she use the words *raven* and *croaks?*
   b. What does "unsex me" suggest?
   c. What are "compunctious visitings of nature"?
   d. What is the meaning of the metaphor, "blanket of the dark"?

6. Note how Macbeth and Lady Macbeth greet each other. As a modern director of the play, what might you add to their greeting? (Suggestions of physical love) Why didn't Shakespeare add it to the text? (Considered inappropriate on stage; also, men played women's roles)

7. What does Lady Macbeth mean when she says, "O, never/Shall sun that morrow see"?

8. What does she mean when she says, "Look like the innocent flower,/ But be the serpent under it"? How does this further enhance the "fair is foul and foul is fair" theme?

9. Using lines from the scene, write your impressions of Lady Macbeth. Teacher circulates to assist and examine pupil writing.

Homework

1. Read Act I, Scenes 6 and 7.
2. Answer the following:
   a. How does the appearance of Macbeth's castle advance the "fair is foul and foul is fair" theme?
   b. Paraphrase Macbeth's soliloquy.
   c. Record and explain lines you feel Lady Macbeth uses effectively to convince Macbeth to kill Duncan.
3. Define: frieze, shoal, chalice, warder.

Aim: What fears and reservations does Macbeth have about assassinating Duncan?

Objective: Pupils will write a paragraph on Lady Macbeth's effect on Macbeth's wavering attitude.

1. What does the word *vascillate* mean? To whom does it apply in *Macbeth?* Have you read other literature in which characters vacillate? Has it ever happened to you?

2. What is there about Duncan that causes Macbeth to waver? (Teacher elicits: Duncan has an unsuspecting nature. See lines in Scene 6 that show a false sense of security in the appearance of Macbeth's castle, furthering the "fair is foul and foul is fair" theme. Also, reference should be made to the line of the soliloquy: "Besides, this Duncan/ Hath borne his faculties so meek, hath been/So clear in his great office, that his virtues/Will plead like angels, trumpet tongued, against/ The deep damnation of his taking off.")

3. What else is there that causes Macbeth to waver from his original thoughts of assassination? Pupils are called on to read their paraphrases of the soliloquy.

4. What is a soliloquy? Why do people make them? Teacher reads soliloquy and asks the following questions:
   a. What does the metaphor, "trammel up the consequence" mean?
   b. What does "We'd jump the life to come" mean?
   c. What "even handed justice" does Macbeth mean?
   d. What reasons does Macbeth offer for not wanting to kill Duncan?
   e. What is the single reason he offers for killing Duncan?

5. Medial summary: What impression of Macbeth do you now have?

6. What happens when Lady Macbeth discovers Macbeth alone and away from his guests? What arguments does she make?

7. Teacher reads scene between Lady Macbeth and Macbeth and asks the following questions:
   a. What is personified in the line "Was the hope drunk . . ."?
   b. What does "Letting 'I dare not' wait upon 'I would' " mean?
   c. What lines can you find that suggest whether or not the Macbeths have children?
   d. What does Lady Macbeth say she will do to the guards?
   e. What does "Bring forth men children only" mean?

8. Write a paragraph discussing Lady Macbeth's effect on her husband. Teacher circulates to assist and examine pupil writing. Pupils may read their responses if time permits.

Homework

1. Read Act II, Scenes 1 and 2.
2. Answer the following:
   a. What line does Banquo deliver in Scene 1 that suggests the "fair is foul and foul is fair" theme?
   b. What does Macbeth tell Banquo to "throw him off the track"?
   c. Paraphrase Macbeth's soliloquy.
   d. Record lines that show Lady Macbeth's fear.
   e. What metaphors does Macbeth create for sleep?
   f. What step does Lady Macbeth take that Macbeth refuses?
3. Define: repose, augment, palpable, gout, stealthy, surfeit, gild, multitudinous, sacrilegious, warrant, predominance.

Aim: How are Macbeth and Lady Macbeth affected the night of the murder?

Objective: Pupils will write a paragraph predicting what will happen after the discovery of Duncan's body.

1. What is the name of the psychiatrist who held that dreams had significance to peoples' lives? Why do you believe people have nightmares? How does a nightmare differ in appearance from real life? If a moviemaker, for example, wanted to show the audience that a character was in the midst of an awful dream, what are some techniques that might be used?

2. What did Shakespeare use in Act II of *Macbeth* that help make it seen like a nightmare? (drunken sleepers, hallucinations, darkness, references to blood and use of the word *blood*, mention of ghosts and night predators).

3. The act begins on the "fair is foul and foul is fair" theme. What line does Banquo say that suggests this theme? What does he give his son to hold on page 22?

4. What does Macbeth say on page 23 to keep Banquo comfortable?

5. What does Macbeth hallucinate? Why? Pupils are called on to read their paraphrasing of the soliloquy, "Is this a dagger . . ."

6. Teacher reads soliloquy and asks the following questions:
   a. Why does Macbeth soliloquize here?
   b. Which lines show that he is very nervous?
   c. Why is such a great warrior, who has killed so many, in such a nervous state?

7. In the second scene we see Lady Macbeth equally nervous. Why? How can we tell? Teacher writes on board:

Lady Macbeth the Night of the Murder

   a. She has drunk wine to calm herself
   b. She is startled by every small noise
   c. She attempts to convince herself she is not nervous
   d. She offers a feeble excuse for why she didn't kill Duncan herself

8. Medial summary: What have we learned thus far about each of these characters' emotions?

9. Macbeth, on returning from the murder, fears he will never sleep again. Why? What does he say is so precious about sleep? Teacher writes on board and reads Macbeth's lines on page 26:

Macbeth's Sleep References

a. Sleep is innocent
b. Sleep cures the day's problems
c. Sleep is the death of each day's life
d. Sleep is the cure for hurt minds
e. Sleep is the second greatest gift
f. Sleep is the chief nourisher of life's enjoyment

10. When Macbeth refuses to return to Duncan's room, what does Lady Macbeth do?
11. Based on their behavior in these scenes, write a paragraph that anticipates their behavior once Duncan's body is discovered. Teacher circulates to assist and examine pupil writing. If time permits, pupils may read answers aloud.

Homework

1. Read Act II, Scenes 3 and 4.
2. Answer the following:
   a. Count the number of blood references in the act
   b. Make a list of animals and insects that are mentioned
   c. In what state is the porter? What is significant about his saying he is Hell?
   d. Why does Macbeth kill the two guards?
   e. Who is blamed for the murder? Why?
   f. Why does Lady Macbeth faint? Who refused to go to Macbeth's coronation? What problem might this cause?

Aim: Why is Act II of Macbeth a living nightmare?

Objective: Pupils will write a paragraph discussing how Shakespeare's writing technique helped give the act the impression of a nightmare.

1. What did Europeans believe about their kings? (Elicit: Divine right)
2. Therefore, what type of offense is being committed by assassinating a king? (Elicit: Sin against God)
3. What has Shakespeare done to establish a nightmarish atmosphere in the act in which God's anointed is murdered? Teacher writes on board:

Nightmare in Act II

a. Nineteen blood references or uses of the word, *blood*
b. Animal imagery: Raven, wolf, owl
c. Evil spirits
d. Sounds of shrieking, knocking, funereal ringing
e. Drunken stupor
f. Evil omens; strange occurrences
h. Horrible, stormy weather

(Pupils refer both to the text and to their homework in developing the preceding answers.)

4. Medial summary: Why has Shakespeare written all these into this act? (Elicit: To imply in part God's vengeance for killing the anointed king and in part evil spirits' joy in destroying the sanity of the world)
5. Teacher reads Act II, Scenes 3 and 4 and asks the following questions:
   a. Why did Shakespeare make the porter drunk, ridiculous, and laughable?
   b. What does Lennox report about the night?
   c. What reason does Macbeth give for killing the guards?
   d. Why does Lady Macbeth faint?
   e. Why do Malcolm and Donalbain run away?
   f. What awesome occurrences do Ross and the old man discuss? Why did they occur?
   g. Who is not going to attend the coronation? How might this be perceived?
6. Write a paragraph that considers Shakespearean technique in producing a nightmare with "merely" the written word. Teacher circulates to assist and examine pupil writing. If time permits, pupils' answers may be read aloud.

Homework

1. Read Act III, Scene 1.
2. Answer the following:
   a. What does Banquo suspect? What tone underlies his brief soliloquy?
   b. Why has Macbeth come to despise Banquo? Paraphrase his soliloquy, "To be thus is nothing . . ."
   c. How does Macbeth persuade men to assassinate Banquo?
3. Define: posterity, oracle, indissoluble, buffet, dauntless.
4. Study for exam on Acts I, II, III, and vocabulary.

Examination on *Macbeth*, Acts I, II, III

I. Identify the speaker of each quotation and interpret the quotation's meaning. (80 points)

1. Yes/As sparrows eagles, or the hare the lion./If I say sooth, they were/As cannons overcharged with double cracks, so they/Doubly redoubled strokes upon the foe.
2. Good sir, why do you start and seem to fear/Things that do sound so fair.
3. This supernatural soliciting/Cannot be ill; cannot be good.
4. There's no art/To find the mind's construction in the face./He was a gentleman on whom I built an absolute trust.
5. Yet do I fear thy nature./It is too full o' the milk of human kindness/To catch the nearest way.
6. Besides, this Duncan/Hath borne his faculties so meek, hath been/So clear in his great office, that his virtues/Will plead like angels, trumpet tongued against/The deep damnation of his taking off.
7. When you durst do it, then you were a man.
8. Sleep that knits up the raveled sleeve of care,/The death of each day's life, sore labor's bath/Balm of hurt minds, great nature's second course,/Chief nourisher in life's feast.
9. If a man were a porter of hell gate, he should have old turning the key.
10. If there come truth from them/(As upon thee, Macbeth, their speeches shine),/Why, by the verities on thee made good,/May they not be my oracles as well/And set me up in hope? But hush, no more.

II. Vocabulary: Define each underlined word as used in the context of the sentence. (20 points)

1. For brave Macbeth . . . with his brandished steel/Which smoked with bloody execution/(Like <u>valor</u>'s minion), carved out his passage/Till he faced the slave.
2. Into the air and seemed <u>corporal</u> melted/As breath into the wind.
3. And oftentimes to win us to our harm/The instruments of darkness tell us truths/Win us with honest <u>trifles</u>, to betrays/In deepest confidence.
4. My thought . . . shakes so my single state of man that function/Is smothered in <u>surmise</u> and nothing is/But what is not.
5. I'll be myself the <u>harbinger</u>, and make joyful/The hearing of my wife with your approach.

6-7. Hie thee hither/That I may pour my spirits in thine ear/And
chastise . . . /All that <u>impedes</u> thee from the golden round.

8. Come, thick night/And pall thee in the <u>dunnest</u> smokle of hell.

9. This even handed justice/Commends the ingredients of our poison-
ed <u>chalice</u>/To our own lips.

10. 'Tis much he dares,/And to that <u>dauntless</u> temper of his mind/He
hath a wisdom that doth guide his valor.

Penalties will be given for writing that abandons basic writing fundamentals. (For example, a pupil may lose as many as 10 credits for aban-
doning basic writing skills.)

Aim: How has Macbeth's conscience begun to affect him?

Objective: Pupils will write a paragraph predicting further signs of decline in Macbeth.

1. Teacher places the following line on the board for class interpretation:

   But this blow might be the be-all and the end-all here.

2. What evidence have we already encountered that tells us that Macbeth will not be able to live comfortably with the deed? (Elicit: His vacillation, killing the guards, his line, ". . . multitudinous seas incarnidine . . .")

3. What do you anticipate will happen to his relationship with Banquo? Why? (Elicit: Banquo heard the witches' predictions; they predicted Banquo would "get kings.")

4. How does Banquo's character compare to Macbeth's so far? What makes him "lesser than Macbeth but greater"?

5. Act III, Scene 1 begins with a brief soliloquy from Banquo. What does it suggest about him?

6. Has anyone discovered any information about Banquo in his or her historical research? (If not, teacher may reveal that Banquo is an ancestor of James I, England's king after Elizabeth I. James I probably saw *Macbeth* performed in the very early 17th century.) What additional conclusion might you draw about Shakespeare's Banquo, based on this information?

7. Why has Macbeth grown to hate Banquo? On page 39 he soliloquizes. What is his mood? Teacher reads the soliloquy and asks the following questions:
   a. What praise does he give Banquo?
   b. What is interesting about the analogy to Caesar?
   c. What is the symbol "barren scepter"?
   d. What does "For Banquo's issue have I filed my mind" mean?

8. Medial summary: Based on what we've seen since the murder, what is happening to Macbeth?

9. Having murdered the king and his guards, Macbeth now plots Banquo's death. Teacher reads dialogue between Macbeth and the murderers and asks the following questions:
   a. What line reveals that Macbeth has spoken to these men before?
   b. Of what has Macbeth been trying to convince the murderers?

c. What excuse does Macbeth offer for not killing Banquo himself?
d. Why do these men obey Macbeth?

10. Write a paragraph in which you predict, with explanation, any further decline in Macbeth's behavior. Teacher circulates to assist and examine pupil writing. If time permits, pupils may read answers aloud.

Homework

1. Read Act III, Scene 2.
2. Answer the following:
   a. Why is Lady Macbeth less happy than she expected?
   b. Suggest two reasons why Macbeth doesn't tell his wife about his plan to kill Banquo.
   c. What is significant about Fleance's escape?

3. Define: assailable, jocund.

Aim: Why has the relationship between the Macbeths lost its closeness?
Objective: Pupils will write a paragraph explaining the deteriorating love between the Macbeths.

1. Teacher writes on board:

   What thou wouldst highly,/That wouldst thou holily; wouldst
   not play false,/And yet wouldst wrongly win.

Who says this? Why? What does it imply about some of the reasons she loves Macbeth?

2. What is trust? How does it occur? Before the murder of Duncan, had Lady Macbeth ever seen her husband do anything untrustworthy? Explain.
3. How has the murder of Duncan affected Macbeth's behavior? What thoughts might he have of his wife now? What may she be seeing in him that she never saw before?
4. Medial summary: Why isn't Lady Macbeth as happy as she may have anticipated?
5. Teacher reads Act III, Scene 2 and asks the following questions:
   a. What does "Why do you keep close . . ." imply?
   b. What does Macbeth mean by, "Better be with the dead," and "After life's fitful fever he sleeps well"?
   c. Why does Shakespeare use animal images such as snakes and scorpions?
   d. Why doesn't Macbeth tell Lady Macbeth of his plan to kill Banquo?

6. The killing of Banquo seems, like the first scene of the play, to be very brief, but it must be played longer. How would that be achieved on stage?
7. Teacher reads Act III, Scene 3 and asks the following questions:
   a. Who is the third murderer?
   b. How are two or even three murderers able to defeat a warrior of Banquo's stature?
   c. What is the significance of Fleance's escape?

8. Write a paragraph that explains why the relationship between Macbeth and Lady Macbeth is deteriorating. Teacher circulates to assist and examine pupil writing. If time permits, pupils may read their answers aloud.

Homework

1. Read Act III, Scenes 4, 5, and 6.
2. Answer the following:
    a. What happens at the banquet to cast suspicion on Macbeth?
    b. How does Lady Macbeth attempt to cover up for Macbeth?
    c. What does Macbeth say he'll do?
    d. Suggest a reason for the insertion of the Hecate monologue.
    e. List the preparations being made against Macbeth.

3. Define: mirth, nonpareil, distill, homage.

Aim: Why does Shakespeare use a ghost to reveal Macbeth's guilt?

Objective: Pupils will write a paragraph suggesting what will happen when Macbeth meets the witches again.

1. Ghosts infiltrate our literature, films, even TV programs. Can you name some? (Examples: *Poltergeist, The Uninvited, Blithe Spirit, Ghost, Topper, Ghostbusters,* even *Dracula.*) What does this suggest about belief in ghosts?

2. How many people in the class believe in ghosts or know someone who believes he or she has had an actual experience with a ghost? What occurred?

3. Has anyone discovered anything about superstitions and ghosts in Shakespeare's England? What were they?

4. Medial summary: To arouse emotion, Shakespeare reduced a mighty warrior like Macbeth to a fearful child by using a ghost. What would you have this ghost look like if you were the play's director? What movements would you have it make?

5. Teacher reads Act III, Scene 4 and asks the following questions:
   a. How does Macbeth react to learning of Fleance's escape?
   b. What metaphor using animals is made to Fleance and Banquo?
   c. Why does Macbeth say, "The table's full"?
   d. How does Lady Macbeth attempt to cover up Macbeth's irrational behavior?
   e. What does Macbeth say he would rather fight than this ghost?
   f. What does it imply when Macbeth says, "And keep the natural ruby of your cheeks/When mine is blanched with fear."?
   g. Who does Macbeth realize was missing from the banquet?
   h. Whom does Macbeth say he'll meet?

6. The scene shifts to the forest in a thunderstorm, where the witches meet Hecate. Because most students of Shakespeare say this scene wasn't even written by Shakespeare and actually detracts from the play, what other use might it have had for Shakespeare to have included it in *Macbeth?*

7. The third act closes with Macbeth in danger. How does Lennox reason that Macbeth killed Duncan?

8. What armies are lining up against Macbeth?

9. Write a paragraph suggesting what will occur between Macbeth and the witches at their next meeting. Teacher circulates to assist and examine pupil writing. If time permits, answers may be read aloud.

Homework

1. Read Macbeth, Act IV, Scenes 1 and 2
2. Answer the following:
   a. What three spirits (images) do the witches show Macbeth?
   b. What three predictions do they make?
   c. Why are the predictions intentionally confusing?
   d. To what new low does Macbeth sink in Scene 2?

3. Define: pernicious, sanctified.

Aim: Why do the witches make confusing prophecies to Macbeth?

Objective: Pupils will write a paragraph on how the evil of the witches affects Macbeth.

1. Have you read any literature in which man does battle with his own evil nature or with evil, would-be corrupting forces? (Teacher might mention Golding's *Lord of the Flies,* Melville's *Moby Dick,* Benet's *The Devil and Daniel Webster,* Marlowe's *Dr. Faustus.)*
2. Describe Macbeth's battle with evil. Does he fight himself? Explain. Are forces outside of himself seducing him to do evil? Explain. Is it both?
3. Who are these witches? What have they shown us? How have their predictions before served Macbeth and the world? How do we know they have power?
4. What is the purpose of evil? What was Satan's goal for the world? (Elicit: create chaos, disorder, pain, etc.)
5. Medial summary: If the purpose of evil is to create pain and chaos and if the witches are evil, what can we predict they will do for Macbeth during his second meeting with them?
6. Why has Macbeth gone to see the witches?
7. What do the witches show Macbeth? Teacher writes on board:

The Witches Show Macbeth

 a. An armed head
 b. A bloody child
 c. A crowned child with branch in hand

What does each symbolize?

8. What do the witches tell Macbeth? Teacher writes on board:

Witches' New Predictions

 a. Beware Macduff
 b. No man born of woman will harm Macbeth
 c. ". . . 'til Birnam wood come to Dunsinane"

9. What can we assume about the predictions? Why have they been given to Macbeth? What theme do the witches once again bring into the play?

10. What new low does Macbeth reach to feel completely safe, in Act IV, Scene 2? Are you fully aware of how awful the scene is? Explain.

11. Write a paragraph on the way the evil of the witches affects Macbeth. Teacher circulates to assist and examine pupil writing. If time permits, pupils may read their answers aloud.

Homework

1. Read Act IV, Scene 3.
2. Answer the following:
   a. Record and explain at least one line that shows Malcolm's mistrust of Macduff.
   b. How does Malcolm test Macduff's loyalty?
   c. Record Macduff's line proving his ultimate loyalty to Malcolm. Explain.
   d. Discuss Macduff's reaction to learning of his family's slaughter. Record the lines that indicate what he intends to do.
3. Define: interdiction, benediction, redress, cistern, impediment, intemperance, imperil, avaricious.

Aim: Will Malcolm be an effective leader for Scotland?
Objective: Pupils will write an evaluation of Malcolm's leadership ability.

1. What are the necessary attributes of a great king? Does Macbeth have them?
2. Who is heir to Duncan's throne? What do we know of him at present?
3. In Act IV, Scene 3, Macduff finds Malcolm to join forces with him against Macbeth. Teacher reads Act IV, Scene 3 and asks the following questions:
   a. What does Malcolm mean by, "To offer up a weak, poor, innocent lamb/T'appease an angry god"?
   b. What does Malcolm do to test Macduff's loyalty?
4. Medial summary: What are your impressions of Malcolm now? Is he worthy to be Scotland's king?
5. We see Malcolm react further when Macduff receives the awful news about the slaughter of his family. Teacher reads the remainder of the scene from line 200 and asks the following questions:
   a. What does Macduff mean by, "And I must be from thence"?
   b. What does Macduff mean by, "He has no children"?
   c. What does Malcolm mean by, "Be this the whetstone of your sword"?
   d. What is your opinion of Macduff's reaction to his family's slaughter?
6. We now know considerably more about Malcolm's character. Write a paragraph evaluating his ability to be King of Scotland. Quote lines from the scene.

Homework

1. Read Act V, Scene 1.
2. Answer the following:
   a. Record and explain the lines that reveal Lady Macbeth's dream.
   b. Write a paragraph of 75 to 100 words explaining the cause of Lady Macbeth's decline from seemingly great strength to her current state of weakness.
3. Define: minute (adjective form), taper (noun form), murkey.

Aim: How has Lady Macbeth changed since the murder of Duncan?

Objective: Pupils will write a paragraph predicting Lady Macbeth's ultimate destiny.

1. How many of you have read Poe's *The Tell-Tale Heart?* What was it about? Teacher recommends Dostoevsky's *Crime and Punishment* for additional study of how guilt affects the human mind and behavior.
2. We are well aware by this time of how Macbeth has suffered. What do we expect Lady Macbeth has felt based on her last behavior at the banquet?
3. Medial summary: In what ways do people behave when their consciences are filled with guilt?
4. Teacher reads Act V, Scene 1 and asks the following questions:
   a. How often has Lady Macbeth been sleepwalking?
   b. Why must she have "light by her continually"?
   c. From her lines, explain what she is dreaming.
   d. What does the doctor mean by, "This disease is beyond my practice"?
   e. What does the doctor mean by, "Infected minds/To their deaf pillows will discharge their secrets"?
5. Teacher calls on pupils to read their homework about the causes of Lady Macbeth's decline.
6. Write a paragraph predicting what will happen to Lady Macbeth by the end of the play. Teacher circulates to assist and examine pupil writing. If time permits pupils may read answers aloud.

Homework

1. Read Act V, Scenes 2, 3, 4, and 5
2. Answer the following:
   a. Record the lines in Scene 2 that suggest problems Macbeth is experiencing while preparing for war.
   b. Why does Macbeth seem overconfident in Scene 3?
   c. What does Macbeth mean by his speech that begins, "I have lived long enough"?
   d. How has one of the witches' prophecies come true in Scene 4?
   e. What does Macbeth's line, "She should have died hereafter," suggest?
   f. Paraphrase the "Tomorrow . . ." soliloquy.
3. Define: epicure, pristine, purgative, sere.

Aim: In what state of mind is Macbeth as war approaches?

Objective: Pupils will write a paragraph explaining the causes of Macbeth's attitude.

1. What happens when you apply something ice-cold to your body? What happens when you leave that cold on the body for 20 minutes or more?
2. How can human problems cause a person to feel a type of numbness? Has such a situation ever presented itself to you?
3. In Act V, Scene 2, there is reason to believe Macbeth is experiencing problems with his men. What lines suggest this?
4. On page 81, which lines express Macbeth's false confidence?
5. On page 82, Macbeth claims his life has "fallen into the sere." What does he mean?
6. In Scene 5, what does Macbeth learn about the cries in his castle? How does he react to the news of his wife's death?
7. Medial summary: What is happening to Macbeth? Teacher writes on board and elicits responses:

Causes of Macbeth's Numbness

a. Loss of respect of subjects
b. Crying of women
c. Death of his wife
d. Decline of Scotland—new civil war
e. False confidence—no need to worry

8. From your homework, read your paraphrase of Macbeth's "Tomorrow . . ." soliloquy. How does it echo his speech "fallen into the sere"?
9. In Act V, Scene 4, a shock is being prepared for Macbeth. What is it?
10. Write a paragraph explaining the causes of Macbeth's mental attitude as war approaches. Teacher circulates to assist and examine pupil writing. If time permits, pupils may read their answers aloud.

Homework

1. Complete *Macbeth*.
2. Answer the following
   a. Why does Macbeth still feel overconfident?
   b. Who does Macbeth kill on the battlefield?

    c. Record Macduff's line that frightens Macbeth.

    d. Suggest at least three reasons why Macbeth loses in combat to Macduff.

    e. Why does Macbeth choose to fight Macduff?

3. Define: clamorous, abhor, vulnerable, tangible, prowess, trenchant.

Aim: To what extent is Macbeth classical tragedy?

Objective: Pupils will write a paragraph considering *Macbeth* as a classical tragedy.

1. Who is Aristotle? About 2,500 years ago Aristotle observed life in Greece and wrote theories based on those observations. He attended the festivals of Dionysus, a god of fertility, where playwrights of the day staged their works. His favorite play, *Oedipus, the King*, a tragedy written by Sophocles, became the standard by which the philosopher judged other tragedies. He set down his observations in *The Poetics*, which has become the standard by which many critics since Aristotle judge tragedy. Teacher writes on board:

   Elements of Tragedy Set Down
   in Aristotle's The Poetics *(in Moxon, 1955)*

   a. There must be universal value.
   b. It must be uplifting in spirit.
   c. A tragic hero must exist, a person of great character with one flaw that helps brings about his or her own downfall.
   d. Fate versus free will must be among the themes.
   e. Catharsis must be experienced: pity for the character and terror for his or her situation.
   f. In decline, the tragic hero recognizes his or her error and reaffirms the goodness of life.
   g. Unities are observed: time (events take place in one day), place (only one set is used), action (plot follows one major complication).

2. We have now concluded reading *Macbeth*. We can easily see that Macbeth experienced a great downfall, from being the second most important man in Scotland to being in a position where he is called a butcher by Malcolm in the play's final speech. Can someone trace the steps of his downfall?
3. What was Macbeth's tragic flaw?
4. Does he redeem himself in any way? Teacher calls on pupils to read their paraphrases of the "Tomorrow . . ." soliloquy.
5. Why does Macbeth refuse to surrender to Macduff? What reasons did you give for Macbeth's loss to Macduff in hand-to-hand combat? Why is Macbeth's head displayed so grotesquely for all to see?
6. Medial summary: What is your opinion of *Macbeth* as a drama? As a learning experience?

7. We've already seen that Macbeth is a tragic hero. Let's examine more closely whether *Macbeth* can be considered a tragedy in the classical (Aristotelian) sense. Using the notes on the board, write a paragraph on the extent to which you believe *Macbeth* is a classical tragedy. Teacher circulates to assist and examine pupil writing. If time permits pupils read answers aloud.

Homework

Expand today's paragraph into a 300-word essay for collection.

After formal lessons on *Macbeth* are completed, a production of the play is presented. A theatrical production, although ideal, is often impractical because of timing, expense, travel arrangements, and so forth. Therefore, a movie version suffices. The famous Orson Welles (1948) production, I found, did not work well for my students despite its widespread fame and critical acclaim. The Scottish dialect added difficulty to the already different Shakespearean language. Moreover, teens today, in general, resent the black and white medium.

Several years ago I discovered the Andrew Braunsberg and Roman Polanski (1971) rendition of *Macbeth*. I have since been showing this version of *Macbeth* to all students who have studied the play in my classes. They seem to enjoy the experience, as they are shocked by the violence and moved to pity the destiny of the main character.

The teacher should note that in both the Welles and the Braunsberg and Polanski productions, directorial liberties were applied. For example, scenes were rearranged, added, or cut. On occasion, a character will speak the lines written by Shakespeare for another. In class, from time to time, a pupil will attempt to follow the script while watching the movie. I always discourage this because it destroys the enjoyment of the performance, and, of course, Shakespeare's original doesn't match either director's artistic choices.

After completion of the film, the 4-day student-made examination process may be applied.

1. On the first day, each group prepares two questions.
2. On the second day, each group prepares and delivers answers to another group's questions.
3. On the third day, the examination is administered.
4. On the fourth day, the examination is returned and discussed for both content and writing skills.

Because the Polanski film has so entranced my pupils, I add questions about the film to their examination to help improve their critical powers of observation and written verbal expression. Such questions may include the following:

1. Was the violence in the film gratuitous?
2. Did the actors satisfy your understanding of the characters?
3. Select at least three scenes that were particularly well done (or badly done—or any combination), describe each, and discuss your reaction to each.

4. Did the Shakespearean language add to or detract from your enjoyment of the play?

In addition, I add a vocabulary question to this final examination on *Macbeth*.

Pupil-Made Examination on *Macbeth*

(Vocabulary questions and the question on the production were constructed by the teacher.)

Essay (80 points): Answer any two of the following questions in at least 125 words each. You may have your texts open, and you will be required to quote lines from *Macbeth* to support your assertions. Each answer is worth 40 points.

1. Discuss the decline in the relationship between Macbeth and Lady Macbeth.
2. Discuss Shakespeare's use of words that make Act II of *Macbeth* seem like a nightmare.
3. Discuss Lady Macbeth's faint. Was it real?
4. Discuss outside influences and their effect on Macbeth's decision to kill Duncan.
5. Discuss the "fair is foul and foul is fair" theme in the play.
6. Discuss the four soliloquies Macbeth delivers during the play.
7. Discuss *Macbeth* as classical tragedy.
8. Discuss what some consider to be gratuitous violence in Polanski's *Macbeth*.

Vocabulary (20 points): Define each underlined word as used in each quoted line.

1. Where are they? Gone? Let the <u>pernicious</u> hour/Stand accursed in the calendar.
2. . . . the truest issue of thy throne/By his own <u>interdictions</u> stands accursed/And does blaspheme his breeds.
3. A great <u>perturbation</u> in nature, to receive at once the benefit of sleep and do the effects of watching.
4. My way of Life/Has fallen into the <u>sere</u>, the yellow leaf.
5. . . . find her disease./And purge it to a sound and <u>pristine</u> health.
6. Thou liest, <u>abhorred</u> tyrant! With my sword/I'll prove the lie thou speakest.
7. As easy mayst thou the <u>intrenchant</u> air /With thy keen sword impress as make me bleed.
8. He only live but till he was a man/The which no sooner had his <u>prowess</u> confirmed/In the unshrinking station where he fought/ But like a man he died.
9. A good and virtuous nature may recoil/In an <u>imperial</u> charge.

10. I grant him bloody/Luxurious, <u>avaricious</u>, false, deceitful/Sudden, malicious, smacking of every sin/That has a name.

Attention must be paid to fundamental writing skills or a penalty will be attached to your score.

Following the examination, 5 or 6 days (depending on class size) need to be provided for pupil performance of their outside research projects. Approximately five pupils can perform each day. My format for such days follows.

1. Create an agenda of speakers.
2. After each speech allow for praise and questions from the audience. (No negative comments are permitted.)
3. At the conclusion of each performance day, pupils may be asked to write what they learned from the information.
4. The teacher should give each speaker an evaluation sheet noting several attributes of the performance and recommending one suggestion for improvement.

References

Attenborough, R. (Producer & Director). (1982). *Gandhi* [Film]. (Available from RCA/Columbia Pictures Home Video, 3500 W. Olive Ave., Burbank, CA 91505)

Beckerman, B. (1962). *Shakespeare at the Globe: 1599-1609.* New York: Macmillan.

Braunsberg, A. (Producer), & Polanski, R. (Director). (1971). *Macbeth* [Film]. (Available from RCA/Columbia Pictures Home Video, 2901 W. Alameda Ave., Burbank, CA 91505)

Bredvold, L. I., McKillop, A. D., & Whitney, L. (1939). *Eighteenth century poetry and prose.* New York: Ronald Press.

Brown, I. (1963). *How Shakespeare spent the day.* New York: Hill & Wang.

Chute, M. (1947). *Shakespeare of London.* New York: E. P. Dutton.

Dowden, E. (1918). *Shakespeare: A critical study of his mind and art.* New York: Harper & Brothers.

Freud, S. (1961). *Civilization and its discontents.* New York: Norton. (Original work published 1930)

177

Fuller, E., & Achtenhagen, O. (Eds.). (1959). *Four American novels.* New York: Harcourt, Brace & World.

Fuller, E., & Klinnick, B. J. (Eds.). (1963). *Adventures in American literature.* New York: Harcourt, Brace & World.

Galvin, C., & Book, C. (1975). *Person to person.* Skokie, IL: National Textbook.

Granville-Barker, H., & Harrison, G. B. (Eds.). (1937). *A companion to Shakespeare studies.* New York: Macmillan.

Griffith, F., Nelon, C., & Staseff, E. (1979). *Your speech* (3rd ed.). New York: Harcourt, Brace, Jovanovich.

Haliday, F. E. (1956). *Shakespeare: A pictorial biography.* New York: Viking.

Harrison, G. B. (1933). *Shakespeare under Elizabeth.* New York: Henry Holt.

Hosley, R. (Ed.). (1968). *Shakespeare's Holinshed.* New York: G. P. Putnam.

Joseph, B. (1962). *Acting Shakespeare.* London: Routledge & Kegan Paul.

Knight, W. N. (1973). *Shakespeare's hidden life: Shakespeare at the Law, 1585-1595.* New York: Mason & Lipscomb.

Markandaya, K. (1954). *Nectar in a sieve.* New York: Harper & Row.

McBurney, J. H., & Hance, K. G. (1950). *Discussion in human affairs.* New York: Harper & Brothers.

Moxon, T. A. (Ed.). (1955). *Aristotle's poetics and rhetoric.* New York: E. P. Dutton.

Muir, K., & Schoenbaum, S. (Eds.). (1971). *A new companion to Shakespeare studies.* Cambridge, UK: Cambridge University Press.

Nagelberg, M. M. (Ed.). (1948). *Drama in our times.* New York: Harcourt, Brace & World.

Ogburn, D., & Ogburn C., Jr. (1962). *Shakespeare: The man behind the name.* New York: William Morrow.

Puzo, M. (1970). *The godfather.* New York: G. P. Putnam.

Raysor, T. M. (Ed.). (1962). *Samuel Taylor Coleridge: Shakespeare criticism* (Vols. 1-2). New York: E. P. Dutton.

Reese, M. M. (1953). *Shakespeare: His world and his work.* Suffolk, UK: Richard Clay.

Reich, C. (1971). *The greening of America.* New York: Random House.

Rowse, A. L. (1963). *William Shakespeare: A biography.* New York: Harper & Row.

Samovar, L. A., & Mills, J. (1980). *Oral communication: Message and response* (4th ed.). Dubuque, IA: William C. Brown.

Sandler, R. (Ed.). (1986). *Northrop Frye on Shakespeare*. New Haven, CT: Yale University Press.

Seigel, P. N. (Ed.). (1964). *His infinite variety*. Philadelphia: J. P. Lippencott.

Shakespeare, W. (1957). *Hamlet*. New York: Simon & Schuster.

Thorndike, A. H. (1928). *Shakespeare's theater*. New York: Macmillan.

Verderber, R. (1994). *The challenge of effective speaking* (9th ed.). Belmont, CA: Wadsworth.

Webster, M. (1942). *Shakespeare without tears*. New York: McGraw-Hill.

Welles, O. (Producer & Director). (1948). *Macbeth* [Film]. (Available from Republic Pictures Home Video, 12636 Beatrice Street, Los Angeles, CA 90066-0930)

Williams, F. (1941). *Mr. Shakespeare at the Globe*. New York: E. P. Dutton.

Wright, L. B., & LaMar, V. (Eds.). (1959). *Macbeth*. New York: Simon & Schuster.